The Way of Truth Eternal
~ Book I ~

MICHAEL EDWARD OWENS

For more information, visit www.thewayoftruth.com.

ISBN: 1-4196-3676-6

Library of Congress Control Number: 2005910439

To order additional copies, please contact us:
BookSurge, LLC
www.booksurge.com
1-866-308-6235
orders@booksurge.com
or,
Amazon.com

Contents

Unless otherwise noted, these are the words spoken directly and verbatim from Sri Leytor, Master of the Order of the Sehaji and co-head of the Grand Council with the great Sage Milarepa.

Chapter One

The Heavenly Hierarchies and Their Structure

The heavens of the Sugmad are governed by the Hierarchies of Masters of the various lines and colors who do work within all the Planes of God's universe to maintain of all order and to guide the fates of man. Within the highest of the dual worlds, what is called the Etheric Plane is the home of the Earthly guardians of the Brown Robes and the Greens. These two Orders do serve of higher powers to keep the forces in balance on Earth and in all the lower planes and planets that do fall within their domain.

On Earth in the pinda or Physical Plane, they do manage of different tasks to keep the forests functioning and the medicinal properties of plants and special animals in good order and maintained. They are held in their highest circle upon the Etheric Plane, for this is the highest place where all natural processes and ways are managed and regulated from.

The Etheric Plane is the closest world of duality to the great heavens of Soul above; and so, it is important that the robes are centered here, for to keep their natural balance, there must be a close link to Soul, that the natural will of God and Its Order are quickly and smoothly conveyed to all those below who are sustained by Its force and presence. These two robed Orders are the only of the angelic host that are headquartered in the lower worlds of God.

The White Robes and the Greys both do have as their true home and headquarters in places and planes that are hidden deep within the upper reaches of God, beyond even the other side of the great Ocean of Love and Mercy where resides the great Sugmad. And so, within this plane there is a great temple where there is kept a great library of all the wisdom and knowledge, as it does pertain to the natural worlds and of their functioning and purpose. The name of this great temple is the Harata Dat Sanwal. It is kept in the city where is found the Golden Wisdom Temple in Arhirit. The guardian of the temple is a Master of the Green line, and his name is Letlanwara. He is an old Soul of great merit who has long guarded the secrets there and does keep of unwanted visitors from entering within its gates.

The Beige Robes are a line with the Whites and Greys that do play an important role within the upper Planes of God's universe. However, within the lower dual worlds very few but the Masters do descend and partake of human forms, for the dual worlds are more strongly driven by the powers of creation and destruction than by those of sustenance, for the Beige Robes do maintain and bring the wisdom and power of the third great line of energy, the neutral power, or sustenance. And so, it is not the intent or necessity in these pages to explain of their role in great detail, for this shall all be taught and said, as it becomes more relevant within the reaches of the higher planes.

The Green and Brown Robes are of an equal Order of merit and authority, though they do serve of different roles. The Green Robes do govern the natural functioning and systems, as they do function within each and every organism below man in the realms of all Its worlds. The Brown Robes do govern of the natural functions and systems as it does relate to interactions between the different species and kinds of creatures. Though this is a subtle difference, it is an important one.

The Greens do guide of developments within the true lines of each branch, and the Browns do guide of progress, as it relates to interaction and the transference of energy of different types and purposes. Though these two Orders do both have of many different functions, these are the primary ones from which do flow all the rest.

The Etheric Plane

The Etheric or Fifth Plane is comprised of many temples and cities of the many different groups and species that do make that place their home. However, there are six primary cities that each is unique in its own way. The first is Arhirit, which you already do know is its name. It does have the great Golden Wisdom Temples where the Brown Robes and the Green Robes reside. This is a city of learning, and many do come there to study or spend time and learn of how the spiritual truths may be revealed or how balance is maintained by the several Orders of Masters who have their Orders headquartered there. The city does have a vortex that is its power and protection, which is located in its center near the Temple of Golden Light. The guardian of the vortex is a noble Master, who is the Lord of that great plane, named, Saguna Brahm. Arhirit is the capital city; and so, the great Lord does reside there to administer of the rest of this vast plane. The offices of government, as well, are housed within its walls, and the peoples and inhabitants are well educated and cultured Souls who do enjoy the life of learning, study, God and the arts.

The second city is the next largest, and Pahrit is its true name. It is a city of industry where the artisans and craftsmen do live and work and perfect of the many practices that are needed by the inhabitants to fulfill their daily needs and wants. The vortex there is protected and maintained by the benefactor of their traditions who is a servant of the Brahm. He is an ancient Master in the Hierarchy and service of the Sugmad, as are all the others, and his name is Bahrana Lam. The temple there is beautiful and well appointed, homage to the skills of those who it does serve, and this great temple of learning and wisdom is called the Preta Rit. It is a temple dedicated to the secrets and harmony of creation in the arts and crafts of those who do toil within the city's walls and of those who do live there.

The third great city is called Prahana Let. This is a city whose population is devoted to those esoteric arts that do sustain the underlying fabric and methods of maintenance of the universe and do serve the labors of the Nine. These are a group of technicians that do have specialized wisdom and learning that does enable them to keep all in its proper functioning, so that no natural systems should become imbalanced or disturbed. The temple there where the Nine do teach is called Temph Le He. It is said as a breath on the tongue and passed lightly over the lips. The temple there is well hidden and difficult to gain access to, save for those of great merit or understanding in the ways of the Sugmad. The Nine and those who serve them are the great Masters and teachers there, and they do maintain of the vortex and its protection and its guardian may not well be named.

The fourth great city of this plane is called Temph Re Ha. It is a city devoted to different pleasures of the sorts that are sometimes found within the various heavens of those who live below. It is a city devoted solely to pleasure and amusement of every form imaginable, and it is only permitted for those who are specially trained to remain within its walls as citizens of its gates. The temple there is where instruction is given in the various ways and means of teaching of others and the visitors of the many varied things to experience and learn that do bring great pleasure to all Souls. The wonders are indescribable and very different in essence and nature than any found on Earth, for what does bring happiness and joy to a Soul in this high region does have no equivalent on Earth. The bliss of this city and the variety of its colors and means does exceed the greatest imagination in the things that can be conceived. The temple of this city is called Prahat Dan Satal. The vortex here is guarded by one of the Brahm's great Order, and his name is Dalar Trewal.

The fifth great city of this plane is called Trelet. Trelet is a city dedicated to the transition of information and travel and movement between the upper and lower planes that do bound the etheric world. All who seek to ascend or go below do come to this way station that the proper protocols and considerations might well be known and understood. The temple here is not for spiritual purposes, but to teach all visiting Souls of the manners, customs and limitations of their travel beyond and within this realm. The station's name on this plane is Teslet, and its vortex and gateways are guarded not by one, but an Order of enforcers who are dedicated to this service. These are Souls who serve the Brahm to protect and serve of his ways, and they are known as the Brahmana

Suta. These are those who bear his mark and do serve to maintain order and governance of all who come and go.

The sixth great city of this plane is called Desrit. Desrit is the other great city that does comprise of the great six, and it is a place devoted to solitude and quiet for those who seek to distance themselves from others or who are new to this fair land. Few are there who long stay here, for it is a transitory place of comings and goings for those who are in between in their understanding and mission or who simply need of rest and time to heal from whatever ails their ways. This is a city of healing, and those who do reside here are well trained in the various arts to accomplish of this end. The temple is dedicated to this purpose, to teach of those who come to give of light and succor to those who are in need. The temple's name is Suktor, and it is guarded by the same who guards the vortex, and his great name is Alakh. This is the guardian of this last great city of the plane of the Saguna Lok.

The Mental Plane

This fourth plane does have of seven major cities that do guide its heart and ways. The first great city is its capital, and it is the home of the Par Brahm. Its name is Brahm Loka, and it is where he does rule from. There is a Temple of Golden Wisdom that is guarded by one of our kind who does serve the unbroken Masters, since the very beginning of time. The city is devoted to the governance of this plane, and all administrators and officials do truly make their homes there. It is also a great place of learning, with many universities and schools, and is well respected and known throughout the many Planes of God. The vortex there is guarded by the great Par Brahm himself, and all Light and Sound and substance do come from within his mouth. Since this Mental Plane is home to thinking, this is a most important place, for the group consciousness of all great universities does have a home and location here. As well, all universities and temples of higher instruction are here constructed and maintained, that the greatest thinkers on Earth and in the heavens do come here to perfect their skills and disciplines and to learn and grow and teach.

7

The second great city of this plane is called Sahret. This is a city purely devoted to the sciences of the many ways of man, and it is here that those who aid of man and his endeavors to understand all material things do here come to study and to learn of hidden secrets. The temple's name is Lei Set and is devoted solely to teaching of material science, and it is well guarded and protected by one of the great Grey Line named Sahren. This is the ancient one who does wield of great power and does manage of the temple and the vortex there to send all great wisdom and knowledge to those who toil below. Those who make their home here are committed to an understanding of the ways of dual forces that do govern the planes below. Some do serve of darkness, and others do serve of light, for it is well understood and recognized that for balance there must be both.

The third great city of this plane is called Senlet. This is a city devoted to medicine and the sciences of the bodies of man and of the creatures, and of all the ways and means to cure the various ailments that do bring pain and suffering below. The temple there for teaching is guarded and protected by one of the White line, and the temple's name is Senret, and the Master's name is Tien (Tie En). The vortex that does govern of the power and wisdom of this place is guarded by another who does rarely show his face. His name is Tsu Psen. He is an ancient Chinese philosopher who ascended long ago from the lands where he was teaching to maintain his current post. His lineage is not well known, or of his past or future, only that he is well hidden but is protected and shielded to maintain the vortex there.

The fourth great city of this plane is called Res Let. This is a great city devoted to language and the communication by word written and spoken, too, and to the signs of expression that do bind of cultures old. The temple here is called Arak Len. It is guarded by a sage of noble standing who has long taught within its halls, and his name is Psen Tsul. The vortex of this city, where it does draw its great power and wisdom to serve all this universe of God, is guarded by one of the Brahm's servants, who does answer only to his Lord, and his name is Selet Brahma. This great city does contain the records of all languages and methods of communication ever known or conceived within the many Planes of God, and those who are able to access of its wisdom shall never be kept from any secrets that lay hidden behind obscure doors.

The fifth great city of this plane is called Pren Lennet. This great city of the mental world is devoted to art and music, for this does have a mental structure as well, and it is here that the spheres do reveal of their perfection to make fine music for the ears. All great musicians past and present have truly passed within these walls, and the completed perfect visions of their great works may be found within its halls. The temple of learning and study here is called Ara Rat. It is guarded by a Master who does answer to the name of Drat Nor. He is one of the noble lines of Whites that have long ago left and gone, yet he does remain to teach of the creative force of love that may be made manifest through the beauty of music and the arts. The vortex of its power is maintained by him, as well, and it is a long guarded secret of the place where it does dwell.

The sixth great city of this plane is devoted to the maintenance and understanding of the development of men and countries and planets, and it is here that great rulers and politicians do come and gather and learn their arts. This city's name is Tokilos, and it does house of many great halls of learning and gathering places, yet the central place and temple of learning is one called Solet Lo. It is guarded by a Master of the long Grey robes of old, and his name is Treylen. The vortex of its mighty power is wielded too, by his hand, and none may approach its awesome power for the fury it does hold.

The seventh and final great city of this plane is called Danwar Katal. This is a great city devoted to the living works of man and other species. It is also devoted to the interactions, contingencies and plans that affect best-laid plans, for there is always certain balance that must be maintained and kept true, and deviations from good planning can result in no good ends. And so, it is the duty of those who toil and study here to understand of the ramifications and options of the many varied courses of action that may be taken in the worlds below to maintain of balance and proper development of the growth of man. The temple and teaching of this plane is by the hands of the Lords of Karma, for this is the place and way that they do teach and understand of their duties and their ways. It is here too that future Masters are trained and made aware of the responsibilities and gifts of compassion that are required for all to be fulfilled. The temple and the vortex are both protected and maintained by these fair lords, yet the temple's name is Lokshor, and it is the true place and center where this great function does occur. These are all the cities and lords and temples and vortexes that are significant in this great plane.

The Causal Plane

There are four great cities of the third or Causal Plane that guides the hearts of man and all actions and deeds performed in his worlds. The first great city is the capital ruled by Brahm. Its name is Brahma Lok. This is the capital city where may be seen all the great Temples of Golden Wisdom and learning, and the records there are also stored in the temple that Shamus does guard. This is a great city well visited and well loved by all who do visit of its walls and wonder of its beauty and majesty. The capital city is dedicated to many things and is an immense domain that encompasses the many varied functions that are required for this plane. It does differ in this manner from the other cities above that do exist and have of a more specialized nature to guide them in their cause. And so, does this city have those in its residence who do serve of governance, educations, records, life contracts and other miscellaneous functions that are required to maintain of perfect balance and function within the lower worlds below. There are too many temples to name them all, and the guardian of the vortex is Brahm himself, who does, through his great love, bring of all energy and power to his and other worlds below.

The second great city of this plane is called Bret Lor. This is a city devoted to the mystical arts of lore and esoteric wisdom that do find a place of power and causation within the worlds below. It is here that those who seek to learn of how to unravel the universe's secrets and the truths of God do come to study with the Masters and seek the answers that are kept here. The main temple of instruction, though there are many others too, is called Mek Le Tor. Though this is a strange sounding name, it is an ancient place long guarded by different Masters who long have left this realm.

10

The current Master who does guard of the vortex there and teach of its secrets and lore is one of the great Grey Line, and his name is Ket Le Nor. He is a noble sage of old and does know of the many secrets of God and truth and does teach them to all who are able to pass within his doors.

The third great city of this plane is called Kep Na Tor. This is a sacred city known for its waters and lakes and beauty and is a place where many do travel to seek of the repose and enjoyment that they do feel they deserve, as a result of earthly good behavior. This is the city and region that does house the many heavens of earthly religions, which do have of limited teachings to lead their students home. This is also the Osgard of the Norsemen and the heavens of the Greeks and Happy Hunting Grounds of the Indians and other old traditions who do maintain of followers and believers who do still cling to their beliefs and achievements of long ago. The temples are unique in kind to each of their different religion's beliefs, and so, each does maintain of their own vortex to feed the flock below of the love and power they do seek.

The last great city of this plane is called Trek Lor. This is a city devoted to the care and maintenance of the dual powers of light and dark, as they are streamed into the other divided worlds below, for the nature of the force and of power in the realms below this plane does differ greatly from those two above and before the Great Divide. And so, this fourth city is the place where these great forces are refined and maintained and created and stored, that those below who wield of their forces may be able to use them for their intended means and for the ends that they do desire. And here too are those Souls trained who do need the skill and power to wield of it below to succeed in their endeavors in this great game of man. And so, the main temple here is called Tret Fer. And the guardian who does manage it and its legions is called Tret Tor, and this is the fourth great city of this plane.

The Astral Plane

The great cities and temples of the second or Astral Plane are many, though of smaller size and power than those of the heavens above, for this is the plane closest to Earth, and power and wisdom

11

are more fragmented here than in the other realms of the Sugmad. But I shall give to you the top five for consideration, and those who do seek of greater knowledge of this matter may seek me where I do reside and teach.

The first great city of this plane is called Anda or Turiya Pad, and its ruler is called Niranjan. This city is dedicated to his organization and government, for it is necessary to have a great host of Souls to maintain of the complicated matters that are required to govern a place such as this. The higher planes are cleaner and less complicated, and so, require less governance and oversight than do those of the astral worlds, for the Souls here are less developed and less able to maintain of proper behavior and actions. And so, this great city is devoted to the governance and protection of the other cities and Souls who do reside on this plane so near to physical existence. The temple here is where the Lord Niranjan does officiate his court and matters of state called Neranjala. This is the name of his temple and palace and it is he who does guard the vortex of power and distribute of its warmth and light to all Souls in existence in his plane.

The second great city of this plane is called Narat. This great city is devoted to those arts and pleasures that do comprise the lower heavens of Earth's religions, and those places where there is hope and warmth to be found for those who have done of good deeds on Earth and are in need of temporary rest and respite and learning before soon returning to Earth in another shell to continue with their lessons. This is a city and way station where good acts are rewarded to those who know not enough nor possess the merit to ascend to higher realms, yet do need of the encouragement and further training to briefly catch their breath before returning to continue on their way. The temple here is a place of golden light and love and it is called Narlat Tre. This is not the Temple of Golden Wisdom, but it is a temple devoted to light and learning and rejuvenation, and the guardian here is called N' lepal. His name is difficult to say in modern everyday language, for he does come from a time and place with an ancient and proud lineage. He is one of the early Masters who brought of man to Earth in the time of the Hyperboreans, when man's Soul was still a mist in the ethers and he was just a dream floating in the hem of God's great cloak.

12

And so, this Master of the Grey Line has long remained to watch over his young charges, as they do learn and grow and finally go on to other places. He is the Master who maintains the vortex there and is responsible for its teaching of the secrets that are needed to succeed in the worlds below.

The third great city of this plane is called Teret Ya. This is a city devoted to re-education and discipline of those Souls who have failed in their lessons to achieve of their mission and goal while in their last time on Earth or other planets. This city is the way station to remit of payment for past errors of judgment and creation of negative karma and to be taught and learn the lessons which were failed while in the physical shell. For if man does not have the vision and prescience to see and learn what is needed while in the physical body, then it does become necessary to take a more direct approach to adjusting for the matter, that the efficiency and balance of the universe might be maintained.

To have a physical shell is a grace given to Soul, that through its free will and wisdom it might make of proper choices to succeed in its endeavors. Yet if this grace is abused and poorly utilized, then there are other ways and measures to address the issues, which were not faced, that the Soul might continue in its development and unfoldment. The great temple of this city is called Peren Te Let, and it is guarded by one of the ancient Grey Line who is called Perel Nor. He does maintain the vortex there and does work closely with the Lords of Karma to ensure that each Soul does learn and receive of the just rewards of its merit or lack thereof.

The fourth great city of this plane is called Net Le Por. This is a city devoted to the administration of matters within the Physical Plane and the government of all structures from within the astral realm that do have and do influence of their counterparts on Earth. The Astral Plane is so vast that its governance is divided into two sections, those relating to astral concerns and of the planes above, and those that are tied to physical counterparts and the structures and developments there. And so, the first great city is more devoted to internal matters and the fourth city to those below. In this city do reside the delegations and representatives of all the Physical Planets and countries and peoples, and it is here that

13

physical policy, treaties, strategy and developments are all negotiated and decided. The grand temple of meeting and gathering is called Unitem Brevi. It is managed and overseen by the Lord and Master Wen Lu Lek. He is an ancient sage and Master who is well skilled in managing and maintaining of the many varied vortices that do connect to all the physical realms that are managed and directed by those who come to meet and collaborate in this great city of the Niranjan.

The fifth great city of this plane is called Pel To Let. This is a city well devoted to the physical matters and movements within the natural structures and bodies of the Earth and other planets, for these material bodies of inhabitation do have a consciousness and karma of their own as well. And so, it is the responsibility and duty of those within these walls to manage and protect of the physical evolution and development of the Earth and other planets. The Master of this city is called Bran Lanat. He is one of the old Grey Line that now is responsible for the physical universe's evolution and unfoldment. The main temple of administration here is called Trenet and the vortex is managed by this same Master who oversees of all the physical realms.

These are the great cities and temples of the Astral Plane. Now we shall continue with the physical.

The Physical Plane

Within the physical realm or first plane there are three additional cities and temples of importance to the ones already mentioned and given in the other works of The Way of Truth. The most important is the city constructed in Africa that is called Ekere Tere. This is the gift of the Living Sehaji Master to the many peoples of Earth to guide them through the end of the Kali Yuga and until the cycle has been completed. It is ruled by a Master called Treylen. It stores all knowledge and wisdom that is known within this universe that relates to the lower planes and the process and secrets of love, growth, unfoldment and all the sciences and material secrets that guide and shape the physical world of man. This new great city was completed in the year 2004. Its power and light have been

14

used to dispel the great forces of darkness that have long ruled that continent there.

The second great city of the Physical Plane is called Tenler. It is located on a planet far away in a different solar system. It is on the planet known as Utelya, which is inhabited by a race not unlike your own, which does strive to grow and learn in the same way that you do. This race may come to Earth near the end of the Kali Yuga, but this is not for certain, for many things and actions are yet to happen that will guide the fate of Earth. This city is devoted to learning and study of the evolution and unfoldment of the hearts and Souls of those within the physical realms, and it is located thus to balance of the power as it is spread within the universe of the Sugmad. For in this physical realm, the duties and functions of the cities and temples do often have of similar function and purpose, but are located in space, time and matter, so as to create a matrix of light and power that shall evenly guide the unfoldment and development of the universe in a balanced and managed way. The Master of this city is one of the Sehaji, and his name is Jeplen. He is an ancient Master of old who long has looked over that corner of the universe and guided the hearts of those living there. He does maintain of the vortex that does bring the light and love of God and does well disperse it throughout the planets and stars that fall within his boundaries.

The third and final great city of the physical world is located in the third corner of this universe of the Sugmad and is called Tretya Len. This is a similar city devoted to light and love and power and balance within the areas of its borders and influence, and it is governed by a Master who is called Tornel. This ancient Master does manage of the vortex and of all within his realm and borders to guide of their development and unfoldment, and it is not the path or true way for those of his kind to ever visit Earth in their physical bodies.

These are the great cities of the Physical Plane that do dispense and govern of the powers of Light and Sound to maintain of balance and love and wisdom within the greatest school of Soul.

15

It is an important thing to truly know and understand the Hierarchy of the heavens, and the cities and guardians there, for as more Souls on Earth do begin to excel in the facility of traveling in the Soul body, then there must be some map and guidelines for the experiences they shall find within the inner realms, lest they do get lost and are found in unspoken of and forgotten places and circumstances that would not well serve of their health and proper unfoldment and development.

The inner worlds to the novice traveler without the protection of the Living Sehaji Master can be a place that is poorly understood and frightening for those who do not know his name; and so, it is well advised to those that desire to travel beyond the body to remember the name of the Master to guide you in your travels. This first chapter of The Way of Truth Eternal, Book I does begin with this topic to familiarize the student with the inner worlds he may encounter upon his travels there, that the experience should be enjoyable and educational, and he should have a better understanding of the truth and beauty and splendor of the many planes and worlds that do exist above his own.

Chapter Two

The Path of God and the Lines of Unfoldment

The path to God is a matter to be found and examined with greatest diligence by those true seekers of His heart and wisdom, for there are many steps and many sideways paths that do appear to lead to higher places, yet which may long delay the true aspirant who hungers only for the great heart and love of God. And so, it is truly important that the student finds the proper way and understands the lines of unfoldment and how they function and affect the progress and success of the seeker. To understand better of this issue and its considerations, it is important to begin with the first critical question: How can one find a path to God?

The path back to God is an individual experience and decision for each who sets upon its journey, yet there are major roads that have been paved and well traveled that may make the way and understanding easier to find and behold. The first step in the process to find a path to God is to first determine of the goal of your quest. Do you seek to reach the highest peaks, to stop midway and rest, to merely escape the clutches of the wheel of reincarnation within the physical and dual worlds below? And how dedicated and committed is your heart to the path that you do choose? For all of these are factors in the decision to be made.

A true path to God does have of certain characteristics that set it clearly apart and identify of its veracity and worth. It must comprise of the essential elements of love, power and wisdom as the trinity of its teachings and techniques to return the Soul to God. Love is the key that unlocks of higher realms, power is the strength to climb the stairs to heaven, and wisdom is the sight and

17

knowledge to understand the proper way to proceed once the gates of heaven are won. Each is a key component and factor in the journey back to God, and any path which does not address an aspect of these three in its teachings will not lead you home with the haste and directness you do desire.

The other critical element that the true path must possess is an understanding and model of the inner planes and bodies of the universe and man that does serve as a map and guide to allow the student to well evaluate his progress and his goals, for if the seeker cannot ascertain where he is, then it is truly difficult to know where he is going or when, or if, he has arrived. And so, the wise seeker who is searching for the path to follow would well keep in mind these things mentioned and bring them to his heart and into his consideration, when evaluating a true path back to God.

For each seeker who walks on Earth there is but one path that is best suited to his needs and abilities at any given moment in time. And it is truly said that two Masters cannot be served simultaneously by the same Soul upon his quest for God; and so, the question is how to determine, what is the true and best path that is fitted to the self of the seeker in this life? The only way which this great question may be answered is through the heart. The mind may aid in the preliminary analysis of the different factors already mentioned as conditions for success of a true path back to God, but only the Soul, while speaking through the heart, may well inform the human consciousness of the true best one to follow to succeed in its desires.

And so, the aspirant, after an initial evaluation of the merits of the path considered, must enter into quiet contemplation and gently ask within to know and hear of which path is the best to aid him on his journey. Sometimes it may be necessary to try and read and compare of different elements of the practice and teachings that different paths do offer, and many times one path may be attempted for a short while and then abandoned in search of a better fit. Yet the most important consideration to know and remember is that when one true path is found and encountered, then the heart shall give such a shout of recognition that there shall be no question in the matter as to which is the best way to proceed.

18

And so, this is the way to successfully evaluate of what is the proper path and teachings for your one true self.

A line of unfoldment is a path of energy that has been solidified and anchored within the heavenly realms, that it has created a stable course and path to follow for those seekers of its teachings and ways. Masters and accomplished Souls of each path and line of unfoldment have traveled on its roads and Mastered of its secrets and well maintain of its corridors and energy that others might follow in their steps. The lines which are maintained and guided do differ in several respects and different characteristics. Different lines do have different trajectories and ending points within the inner planes and each line has its own frequency and vibration to attract or repel certain Souls from its doors, depending on their readiness or merit. And so, there are major lines associated with the major phases of development of Soul and also with the missions and duties within the heavenly hierarchies that do guide the development and unfoldment of man and all the worlds of the Sugmad.

Within this universe there are four principal lines of unfoldment that are guarded and maintained by the Orders that do guide their works. The first is the White Robes, and this line of energy is called Telnor Et. This is a positive, creative energy of birth and emancipation and it is comprised of the several hierarchies that fall within its domain and authority. This is a high path of development, and its line of unfoldment does have a steep trajectory and rapid velocity of ascension from within the Earthly plane.

The second are the Grey Robes, and this line of energy is called Trek Len Lor. This is a vortex of energy that does stem from and serve of the negative powers of destruction and illusion, and it is a complementary line to the first to keep of proper balance within the lower worlds of the Sugmad. It is comprised of its hierarchies and orders that do serve of its greater purpose and structure to do its duties here. It is also a line steeply angled to the heavens with a strength and power equal to the Whites to balance of their force and ways.

The third major line of unfoldment is the Green Robes. This is a lower line of unfoldment with a trajectory less steeply angled and with less power and velocity, and it is a path devoted to safely bearing Souls within the lower planes to various destinations as they do serve the various Orders and learn the lessons that are needed. This line is called the Nor Al Ten.

The fourth great line of energy and unfoldment is guided by the Order of the Brown Robes, and this lower line of trajectory and power does parallel the Greens within the lower worlds to provide of balance in the powers of their functions and energies. This line is called the Tor Tre Let.

An extension of each of these lines of energy about which little can be revealed is that of the Lavender Robe. This Robe, a highly secret Order, operates at the direction of the Most High, beyond even the range of the Sugmads and the Silent Ones. Members of this Robe follow the directives of the Living Sehaji Master and those whom he designates. They operate at his beck and call to serve a purpose that only he shall know. It can be said that those who are members of this Order will act to protect the Sugmad and the worlds below from all dangers, including those above and below who would disrupt the destined journeys of Soul to God. Not much more can be written but will be revealed to those whose spiritual path and destiny brings them to the Lavender Robe.

And so, these are the four primary lines of unfoldment and their different Orders and characteristics that do penetrate the heavens of the worlds of the Sugmad, and their many branches and derivations and arms do create and maintain of the varied paths and teachers that all fall under their hierarchies and authority. And so, the aspirant on the path is well to understand of where and how the teachings he does seek and trust do fall within the scale of the given paths to God and their effectiveness and validity.

Each Soul upon the Earth does serve of one of the great lines of unfoldment, either the Whites or Greys or Greens or Browns, for every Soul must have a line and energetic path within which they do fall. Even if they are so fortunate to be inducted into the Lavender Order, it will be the result of the training they did receive

20

in one or more of the other Robes. And so, as Soul commences on its journey through the many lifetimes in the lower realms, it does select and switch back and forth between the different lines and pathways to garner the experience and knowledge of the different lines of force and how they do work and function. And further in its journey along the path and closer to God-Realization, Soul does select of the White or Grey or Beige Robes to be its permanent affiliation of service for the future of its assignments and endeavors, though this is not to say that never shall there be changes, for a Soul may temporarily decide to switch for a given period to better learn and understand the ways and finer points of truth and wisdom as it does relate to the other line and power.

All the world's religions do fall within and answer to some higher authority or path along the great lines of unfoldment that have already been mentioned. However, it is not the course of these teachings to provide a means or manner for the misuse of holy information to oppress or judge of others, and for this reason, the major world religions shall be linked to the true path of unfoldment that they do follow, but none shall be placed higher than any other, to prevent of misguided thought and action.

The four great lines of unfoldment, to include the Lavender Robe, and their religions are thus:

White: The Way of Truth, Eastern Mysticism: Buddhism, Taoism, Confucianism, Shintoism, Zen, Yogic Sciences, Unity, Zoroastrianism, Mithraism, the Essenes, Cabala.

Grey: Christian Science, Jehovah Witness, Hinduism, the Way International, Islam, Roman Catholic Church, Greek Orthodox Church, Russian Orthodox Church, Protestant Church, Mormonism, Greek and Roman Polytheism, Nordic Religions.

Brown: Druids, Santeria, Coptic, Latin Tribal, Pagan/Wicca.

Green: Spiritualism, African Tribal, Gaia/Earth Goddess.

Lavender: All of the above.

Though there are elements of the positive and the negative in each of these ways and paths, and some Souls of merit have served of both lines during their past lives and missions, these are the major affiliations of the world's major religions as they do follow the branches and tributaries of these major highways back to God.

It must be understood now that these great lines do share a common root and heritage, for it was from those who created of this universe that these lines were initially drawn and do parallel those of others in the universes beyond the Sugmad. So as the student does work his way along the path, he is well to remember that though each path does appear separate, they are all in reality part of the greater whole, which binds together the very fabric and essence of all the universes of the Great God, for beyond the Sugmad there is a greater One who is the God of All and may be spoken of as the Great God or Nameless One and about which more shall be spoken, when Its wisdom is truly given in the words of Chapter 12. And so, one should not fret or worry of the nature or merit of the path, as it does compare to another, for all paths and lines do eventually return home to the Ocean of Love and Mercy, when the Soul is finally ready for its arrival and may recognize its true home and destination.

First of the White Robes: There are five primary Masters that teach within this line of unfoldment. The first and greatest and the head of all others within this Hierarchy of love and unfoldment is Milarepa. He is the one that guides of all others within this universe's planes, for he does possess the greatest wisdom of all that may be known, except for Dan Rin. Milarepa's specialty is the teaching of all others in the many secrets of God, and long has he given great service to the will of the Sugmad. Though his level of initiation does stretch far beyond this universe, even to the 37th plane of God's heavens, in this universe of the Sugmad he does reside on the twelfth with all other Masters of eminence who are near the heart of God, for none do reside on the thirteenth except for the Silent Nine.

Milarepa heads of all the Councils that do govern the affairs of the lower Orders, and it is his wisdom and grace and power that guides of best-laid plans with the assistance and cooperation of the Nine

22

and the other Orders. He has mastered of all wisdom within this universe of God and may be considered of equal or greater knowledge than even the Nine, though he does submit to their will and dominion while serving within these planes. Milarepa may be found on the twelfth plane by those who are able to go there, though often he does come and teach within the lower realms when there is some matter of importance that does require him to be there.

The second great Master within the White tradition is Yun See. This is an ancient Master who few have ever known or seen, for he does teach in quiet seclusion of the highest of the other Orders and rarely may he be found or heard by any who are not Masters of their path or tradition of teaching. Yun See's area of specialization is the teaching of Masters to guide of all students within their way, for it is a subtle art and skill to bring the great truth and knowledge within the inner planes in a way and format that it well may be understood and seen and followed. And so, this noble Master, who resides on the tenth plane of the Sugmad, does travel within the lower worlds to teach of the light bringers to do their deeds and work.

The third Master of the White line is Senlet. This is also a Master not well known to any of the lower worlds, for his is a duty and mission that must be maintained in secrecy. Of the name Senlet, this is the truth. The Master by this name did long ago study in the temple and did take that as his last name to identify his origin and where he did love to call home. The first half of his name is Leslen. This shall help to further identify him as the Master of his line. Senlet is the one who trains the Red Dragons who do guard the sacred vortices and the bringers of the light. The Red Dragons are those great Souls who have committed themselves to the mission of protecting of the positive force and its various permutations and missions within the worlds of God. They are the balancing measure to the Dark Angels of the Greys who do serve of similar duties within that tradition and great way. Senlet is a Master who resides on the eighth plane, and there in quiet secrecy and toils does he receive of those great Souls who wish to enter into service and does train them in his ways. He also does toil with the Nine and many others to coordinate the activities of his legions that all balance should be maintained. He is a great Soul of noble distinction to whom many thanks should be paid for the services he does offer to protect of those below.

The fourth great Master of this line is Sri Tindor Saki. Sri Tindor is a great teacher of the way of Light and Sound, and he is the one who teaches all others within the Sehaji way and of the White brotherhood and various other Orders who do follow within the path and tradition of the White Robes. Though Sri Tindor is a member of the Sehaji and is the head of their number here, he is also widely known and traveled in the ways of other paths. Often he does appear and speak in many different forms and faces and names to those whom he does seek, yet he is the one of the five that gives of great light and wisdom to those who go below and do truly seek the worlds and truth of God. Sri Tindor may be found on the twelfth plane of this universe, where he does have his home and place, yet most often he does work with Souls on the seventh plane or below, as he is needed and as circumstances do require.

The fifth great teacher of this way is the Angel Gabriel, for he is a great Soul of merit who does coordinate and manage of many of the affairs and plans of the Orders within the lower Hierarchy of the White line within this universe of the Sugmad. Gabriel is a Soul of great merit and well accomplished in his ways and duties, and though his level of initiation does exceed the tenth plane, he does serve within the fifth and below to be within the dual worlds where he must remain to succeed of best-laid plans and the will of the Sugmad.

These are the great teachers of the White Robes and of this path of unfoldment, and their responsibilities and stations. Now onward to the Greys.

There are three great Souls that do govern of the affairs of the Grey Line. The first of these great Masters is the Kal of this universe of God. The Kal is a Master and teacher of all within the negative way and path, and it is his duty and responsibility to see that all is maintained and balanced to match against the Whites and keep of certain balance within this universe of the Sugmad. The Kal must be properly understood to know of his true essence and mission,

24

for it is only within the lower worlds of duality that he does truly reside.

Leytor is the one who does head of the Grey Line and is a great and noble Soul who, like Milarepa, does possess of merit and wisdom that far exceeds this universe and its limited 15 planes. Leytor does possess the wisdom and knowledge of one of the 63rd plane of all the heavens of God that do lie beyond the realm of the Sugmad, and Leytor does in this universe live and reside within the twelfth plane with Milarepa to do his duties there, though his mirrored reflections below are manifested in the many planes that he does rule and guide. And although Leytor does exceed Milarepa in initiations and merit outside this universe of the Sugmad, within Its realms and in the duties and roles that each does fulfill right now, Milarepa is accorded and does wield the greater wisdom and merit in his position as the head of the Grand Council and leader of the Sehaji, for in a lower universe it is the duty and mission for the many planes of learning to be guided and overseen by the powers of the negative force.

And so, though Leytor is a Soul of great merit and profundity and does reside far above any worlds of duality, his service and affiliation is within the great Grey Line, which is responsible for all power and destruction of the negative force of the Great God that does serve to keep of balance within the many universes of Its realms. And so, Leytor does oversee and manage of all within the Grey Line in this universe and in its Hierarchies and Orders who do carry of its works. Leytor does sit in Council with Milarepa and Sugmad and the great Nine to plan and manage of the affairs and efforts of all within this universe of the Sugmad.

Second in command under Leytor within the great Grey Line is Kusulu. Kusulu is a hidden Master and teacher who does truly guide and train of those great Souls who do serve of his legions, which are known as the Dark Angels. These great Souls of enormous merit and wisdom do have the task and duty to enforce of the Grey Line's activities and toils to keep the balance with the Whites, for there is no morality or judgment on the duties they do bear. It is simply a matter of keeping of all balance that the universe should function well and all should be maintained and continued, as it should be. And so, Kusulu does have the task and responsibility to teach of all who go and do of all the duties that fall within the realms and plans of the orders of the Grey way.

The third and final Master who does toil within the Grey tradition is Tenlor. Tenlor is a great Soul who is little known or seen who does have the awesome duty to teach and coordinate of all the Masters and teachers who do fall within the Hierarchy of the great Grey path to God. He is the one who convenes and heads all Councils and calls all others to obey and does give of all their missions and duties to keep the balance met and the best-laid plans of God well placed. Tenlor is a Soul who does reside on the tenth great plane of the Sugmad, though his duties do often take him to within the lower worlds where his power and duties are required to succeed of best-laid plans.

The Master and lord of the Green line and path of unfoldment is Sayneen. This is a Master who teaches and manages of all within her line who do govern of the powers of the lower dual universe of the Sugmad. She does serve of her higher Masters in the Hierarchy she does serve above and is the one who coordinates and manages of all affairs within the dual worlds below. Sayneen is a great Soul who does reside on the fifth great plane of God and does hold her council and affairs in her great temple there.

Of the Brown Robes there is a similar one who answers to the great Tenlor, who is his Lord and Master. This Master of the Browns does, like Sayneen, coordinate of all activities and duties within the worlds below to maintain of certain balance within the worlds of the Sugmad. This great Master is called Treplen. This is a great Soul who long has served this post from within the fifth plane of the Sugmad, and does have as his duties and ways to keep the balance of his Orders within the lower worlds of God's great universe.

Of the Lavender Robe, it shall be known that the head is a Master of undisclosed spiritual development who operates under the direction of the Living Sehaji Master. The wisdom and training he receives comes through the essence of the Living Sehaji Master directly from the Sugmad and the Grand Council. Together, a few gifted Souls shall share the Lavender Robe mission outwardly and the Lavender Robe consciousness inwardly, although the greater burden of that consciousness will be the Abbott's alone. In the time of Dan Rin, they will establish the Brakosani Order for the first time in human history, although the Order still serves in other planes and dimensions beyond the Celestial Seas.

Under the Living Sehaji Master's guidance, they are directly overseen by the Spiritual Council, which is headed by the Living Master's designee, often a Soul of high spiritual note. The Council includes Milarepa and Gabriel, among others, to represent the Sehaji of this Sugmad. They do confer with the Sugmads, and other Orders, to determine what spiritual directives of the Living Sehaji Master still require completion and to await his further guidance.

Though the relationship between the Grey and White and Brown and Green Robes does appear confusing, it is a simple matter to understand. Within the higher heavens the Grey and White Robes are established and do stretch beyond the Sugmad. However, within the lower dual planes of Its universe the Brown and Green Robes were created to do the works and manage the details of all that falls within the responsibilities of the Greys and Whites. And so, Browns do serve Grey, and Greens do serve White, although there may be cross-coordination and collaboration with the Lords of Karma and between the lines, as is necessary and required. And as well, the Grey and White do both function in the lower worlds but at a different frequency and vibration than do the Brown and Green, though they do, as well, serve the same function of their polarity of energy and role to balance of the other and keep all good things in check.

This is all of the great Masters and teachers who do comprise the Hierarchy of the various lines of unfoldment from within the universe here. These Souls are the ones of merit who do toil and labor well to ensure all other matters always do occur in the way that they are needed and necessary to succeed with best-laid plans.

Gabriel, as a member of the White Robe, is the servant of the Sugmad and also does coordinate the efforts of the Kal to do his will and ways; however, he does have special status in the affairs of this universe, and though he does defer to the wishes of the Kal in most matters, he can appeal to the Sugmad if he does believe there is cause that must be considered and addressed. He also does accord equal consideration to the wishes and desires of Brahm, Vishnu and Shiva and the Lords of Karma, though he is not bound to answer to them or heed of their commands or desires. Indeed, it is the opposite situation, for all below the Kal do view Gabriel as his equal and do mind the ways and wishes of his heart and commands, though he is a Soul of grace and light and infrequently does he issue of missives or instructions that do contradict or cause issue with the ways and duties of those within his Hierarchy and command.

Gabriel may well be seen as the light that balances of the Grey Robe of the Kal, and though there does not exist a formal Hierarchy of command, for all Kal's children and the Lords of Karma do fall within the realms of his Grey Line, there still exists the authority to command of all who fall below his rank and merit, though Gabriel would, out of respect and deference, first consult with Kal before taking of any direct action with one within his command and Hierarchy. And so, this is the relationship and structure of Gabriel, who does command of the White Robes within the lower Planes of God within this realm of the Sugmad.

The Lords of Karma (spoken directly and verbatim from the Council of the Lords of Karma)

The Court of our number is located on the sixth great plane of God, where all do come in their Soul body to be judged and to be heard before being sent onward or being returned to some other plane below to begin the next phase of their development and learning and the search for the great wisdom each must gain to finally ascend the peaks of God's heavens and forever make their home above. Twelve sit in our number, and there is also one of the Nine which does come to be the deciding factor when agreement cannot be reached. However, this is rarely the case, for we have only on one or two occasions not been in uniform agreement as to what must be done and said in the instances that do pass before our hearts.

Within the Council we are divided between the Grey and White, six to the left and six to the right, to accomplish of our duties. Those who sit to the left do judge those Souls of the Grey and Brown lineage who come before our table. Those of the right do judge the Whites and Greens who come to us, as well, for none may bear the Beige mantle of the third lineage, except as ascended Masters who are able to well wield of both powers in a balanced fashion and thus do the work of God. Within each of the six from either side, one Lord does have as its area of expertise and specialty each of the first six planes of the Universe of the Sugmad. From the left and far right and moving to the center in ascending order, the Physical, Astral, Causal, Mental, Etheric and Soul Planes are all represented by one who sits and judges and commutes sentence upon those who come and sends them to specific regions or places to do what must be done. In this way all is done in an efficient and timely fashion, and all Souls may quickly be judged and sentenced and sent to the place that they have earned for their next life and experience.

The Lords of our Council are trained by other Masters who have previously served and now do teach at the school, which is in our name and function within the lower planes, for those who do represent and share the wisdom of this duty and responsibility do come from different paths and ways from within this universe of the Sugmad. At the head of the temple of instruction, however, it always is a Master of the Sehaji or one of the Nine who do oversee and manage of all affairs and bestow of the final initiations that are needed and required to finally sit on the Council and serve the will of God. Currently, the Master who is the head of this temple is a little known or seen one who has held this post for the last 10,000 years. His name is Lotan (Lo Tan). He is an ancient Master of old who was trained beneath Kusulu to carry of his deeds and mission so many years ago. However, if Lotan is called away to serve temporarily in other places or duties, then one of the Nine or another Master will come and take his place for short durations of time.

The training for service within our ranks does depend on the experience and abilities of the student. Some who have sat before

29

in our capacity do often return to the Physical Plane for further training and experience as Soul and may serve in a similar capacity within that lifetime there. Upon returning to realms above, they may quickly pass through the training and, once again, rejoin our ranks. Others who do wish to serve for a first time may require of more study, perhaps 500 or 1,000 years, for it does all depend on the Soul and its experience. And it also must be remembered that time does not pass the same within the inner realms. It is elastic and relational; and so, though this may seem an eternity down below, up above it could pass in the instant of an eye, if that was how the Soul did desire it.

The spiritual abilities and gifts that are required to serve this function and role are the facility of quickly reading the Soul records for the individual that does come and the ability to project of different contingencies and scenarios for the future lifetimes to come, to gain for the Soul the experiences it does require, as well as an understanding and ability to see and read the karmic debts and balances, and see how they must be applied generally and to specific other Souls, and a facility and knowledge and thorough familiarity with all the Masters of the inner realms and all the cities and temples and heavens and hells and other places where Souls may be sent to gain the experience they do require.

This is a small overview of the many skills that must be had to serve within our ranks and function well and justly as a member of the body which does mete perfect justice to all who come and stand before our bench and hear what must be said for the next step of their journey back to God.

When a Soul does come before us that has passed off its entire debt and is freed from the great wheel to continue on its way, it is shown to a separate room with a different form and function to select what will be its duties, now that it is freed from the Wheel of 84. This room does appear to have of several screens or walls upon which images and options are shown as to possible places and duties that may be chosen and selected to go and serve of the Sugmad. There is one within this chamber who does wear of our mantle, though he is not one of the 12 who sits and judges Souls. This one speaks to the Soul in question and explains to it the options which may be selected to be done, and after the Soul has made its choice, it merely walks in the direction of the choices it has selected and then it finds itself in that place of service that it has chosen to do. The options it has to choose from are selected from an analysis and knowing of the nature of the Soul and its many lifetimes past, and so, it is a rare occasion that one of the options given is not suitable to it, and in this manner does each Soul move on to greater acts of service and love in the heavens of the Sugmad.

For Souls who have not resolved of all their karma and must return to a shell below within the physical world to continue their education, several options do exist. First, that Soul may be sent to a pleasant place of relaxation to enjoy the fruits of pleasure until the time does come to return below and start again. Second, a Soul may be sent to an unpleasant situation to resolve of a portion of its debt, for if its debt is so large that it never could be repaid in many lifetimes on Earth, then it may be required to repay of some of it above, where physical bodies are not required to complete what must be done. For it must be understood that the Physical Plane is a delicate region with a finite amount of shells and opportunities to descend and learn and grow, and it is a privilege to go and take a shell and learn the lessons, which are needed to aid in the ascent and return to Sugmad's arms.

And so, for those who repeatedly abuse the opportunity and fail to learn their lessons; they are sometimes given time to think in one of the worlds above until they have grown in wisdom and are ready to return to realms below in a physical incarnation. Others still may go to universities or temples to learn and study some skill, which may be needed or desired in the next lifetime to come, and others too who are greatly damaged or traumatized or tired may be put to gentle slumber and moved to a quiet temple to recover and rest and heal until the time does come that they are ready and able to continue on their journey and ways. So these are the major options that Souls do have to take, as they wait for their next incarnation to continue on their way, and it is something that has of many permutations on the general theme, but essentially this is what may be encountered and experienced.

31

For those who cause of significant negative action while in the physical shell, there is a balance to be paid in karmic debt for what has truly been done. The Council does not grant any grace or consideration for the negative deeds of man, for this may only be done by a Master or a savior who intercedes on his behalf, and through his or her position and Mastery of the Holy Spirit does grant that Soul the mercy of the Father through the hands of their expertise. And so, often it will occur that some Master may accompany a Soul and offer to take some karma on its behalf and resolve it into the Life stream, and this is the providence and jurisdiction and right of those of merit, to aid of those who follow them, but it is not something that the Lords of Karma are authorized to do or are able to perform.

Of suicide, this does require special mention, for this is a unique case and circumstance. Those who do take of their own life are granted no reprieve of the conditions that led to their demise. Instead, they are taken to a special temple where they are ministered to and cared for until they have recovered from the trauma and the shock of their untimely ascent to the other side. Then, they are educated and shown to understand the error of their ways and thinking in the last life they did live. And once they have recovered they are sent, again, below to relive the same lessons and experiences that they did fail once before. However, if they should commit suicide, again, and fail again the lesson, then upon subsequent returns the lesson will be repeated with ever increasing severity and intensity until the way is won and the Soul does understand and can continue on the path, for there is no special punishment for this act, save the trouble and inconvenience and annoyance of again having to repeat the circumstances of pain and hurt and suffering which led to the act at first.

When Souls who are waiting to return or have ascended do have time to themselves, they are free to move and travel as the merit of their initiations and the restrictions of their inter-incarnation pause do allow. For those who have ascended, they do have a mission and role to play in the service of God, yet they do have considerable flexibility in their performance of that role and the timing and urgency of their efforts. And so, many do toil with fervor, initially, but may slow and then later resume, as they learn of the possibilities available to them to do and of what they do enjoy and wish to experience. For those who are merely waiting for another opportunity to return to the Physical Plane, they do know that they possess a limited time before their next incarnation, and so, they may explore and travel the plane or city or temple where they have been sent to wait in the interim. And so, there are many options of things to do and see, and it is found by most to be a very pleasurable experience, except perhaps by those who are repaying a terrible debt for the ignorance of their mistakes and the karma they have created.

Chapter Three

The Vision of the Master

Leytor (spoken directly and verbatim)

The Masters of the Sehaji differ from all others in several important ways. First, the Sehaji are the most powerful of all the Masters within this universe of the Sugmad, and they do possess the greatest wisdom, power and truth of any who do serve within the established hierarchies and lineages of God. This is not to be confused with the Silent Nine, for they are not an Order who do descend into a physical incarnation to serve within the Physical Plane or who do tutor Souls within the inner worlds, for this is not their duty and place, and their merit and authority may exceed that of a Sehaji Master, or it may not, depending on the Master in question. The power and merit of the Nine, however, do always exceed that of all other robes. And so, though the qualities of power, truth and wisdom are three that do differ in magnitude and scope from that of other Masters of different robes and traditions, this is not the only thing that does set the Sehaji apart.

The Sehaji do require of extensive training in a greater variety of arts of the inner realms and of expertise that does pertain to the mechanics and issues of a higher Order than that of other robes. For example, a Master might be concerned with the construction of a spiritual city or the consciousness of the globe or the universe or any other broad and tremendous scope of matters of importance to the higher development of man and the balance of the universe. And a Master of another robe might be concerned and deal with issues of a more secular nature, such as feeding the poor or doing works of public service or issues within the psychic realms than with the pure truth of God. That is to say, the Sehaji do answer to, and have a responsibility for, issues and problems of a higher nature that do relate to the timeless and pressing concerns of Soul.

This is not to belittle or lower the respect accorded to those of other paths, for they are true and necessary and important steps along the path, for can you say that the teachers of the primary grades of school are more or less important than those of later levels? Indeed, one cannot successfully function well without the other, and each does play an important part in the role and responsibility each does have. However, for those who have reached the final leg of their journey and do seek the highest truth of God, the Sehaji are those who have had the valor and courage to go and seek this truth and pass it on to those who follow them. So it can be said that the difference between the Sehaji and the others is the area of expertise and breadth and depth of wisdom that must be acquired and possessed to earn this rank and merit, however, this never should be confused or said to be more important than any other, for this is not the case.

The Living Sehaji Master is the highest level of achievement within this universe, and this rank and title does give to him the ability and authority to command of all others save for the Sugmad. However, no Living Sehaji Master would wield the power in this manner unless it were a condition and case of dire emergency and threat to the balance of the universe, for that would not be the way of love. The Living Sehaji Master, when he or she does wish to address of some concern or issue, which falls within the Hierarchy of another Master or Order or Council, would first go to the head of that Order out of courtesy and respect for the authority and position of the one who has earned that place. Then, the Master would raise of his concern or issue and ask for the advice or assistance of the one he does address. After receiving the wisdom and sharing of the other Master, a dialogue of understanding and respect does ensue in which the matters are discussed and hopefully resolved. And if one of the lower rungs of another Master's domain is required, then that Master would call to his or her own, or give permission to the Living Sehaji Master to call to them directly, to resolve what needed to be said. In this way are balance and harmony maintained and all does function well and smoothly. For one of the tests to receive and wield of ultimate power is how you do act and relate to and treat of those who do stand before you and must answer to your will and ways, for there is no merit in the tyrannical use of power, if it does violate the free will of another who seeks to do the duties of his rank and area of responsibility.

And so, after a Living Sehaji Master has developed a familiarity and relationship with the head of another line or Hierarchy, afterwards permission may be granted to, in future cases, call directly to the one that he does seek. However, this would only be the case after permission had explicitly been granted from the other Master of the authority and rank who could make the offer for that line. And in this manner, harmony and balance are achieved and truth and love and wisdom are passed downward within the different ranks and robes and hierarchies that do govern and manage of all functions within this universe.

Mastery in The Way of Truth is first experienced at the tenth plane of the Sugmad, and does increase until the seventeenth, which is the highest that is possible presently to achieve within the Sugmad's realms, for this is the mantle of the Living Sehaji Master. And so, after the tenth plane the initiations are granted with the accumulation of experience and the passing of tests and challenges up to the fifteenth level, and there all Masters do generally remain except for the Living Sehaji Master and those few admitted to even higher levels. The sixteenth plane is a plane of rest and repose for the Living Sehaji Master, and few may enter there save those who the Living Sehaji Master does ask to share some time with him or consult on specific issues or concerns, for the Living Sehaji Master may lower to the thirteenth plane if the Rod of Power is temporarily given to another to hold in his stead and place or there is some other reason why he may not hold the Rod but is not yet ready to pass it on to the next in his line. And so, from the tenth to the fifteenth, the Living Sehaji Master and those with these Circles do learn to wield the God-power, what are its characteristics and abilities, the other Hierarchies and Councils and beings of the inner planes and of the hidden esoteric secrets of the universe, which do allow them to assist the Living Sehaji Master to perform his duties and serve the will of God.

In the physical body, the Living Sehaji Master is faced with many challenges and hurdles along the way to this destination, for to be a Master of the Sehaji is to be a pure channel for the Light and Sound of God and this cannot be done if the inner bodies do contain of any impurities or dross. And so, the Living Sehaji Master in his training and along the way does face of many challenges and difficulties, which must be overcome to remove all densities from the inner shells so that nothing does impede the light and flow of God-power from above. These could include physical illness, emotional trauma, financial difficulties, problems with the home or car or others in his circle of associates and friends, lack of clear direction and purpose, manifestation of things or objects that are outside of his life mission, loneliness, isolation, difficulty relating to and being understood by others, and many other things, which do relate to removing all obstacles to the flow of pure power from the highest Planes of God's heart. However, once Mastery is accomplished, all of these may go away, for now the Soul is a Master and in complete control of all that does surround and affect him, and so, any discomfort or difficulty that is experienced is only done by choice and with the knowledge and understanding of what are the reasons and purposes for the action that is done.

It must also be understood that the process of achieving Mastery has almost nothing to do with the amount of time spent in The Way of Truth, while within the physical shell in this lifetime. It does truly most depend on the experience and merit gathered in the many past lives that did precede the one being currently lived. And so, in this lifetime, it could be done in as little as two-and-a-half years, although this would be a rare occasion indeed, or as long as 25 or 30 or more, depending on the particular circumstances and conditions that did accompany the Soul in its lifetime here on Earth. The one thing is this: The second initiation must be achieved before the ability to freely and widely travel in the inner worlds is granted, no matter what the merit of the Soul. And at this time the course of study within The Way of Truth does require of two years to reach this level of achievement, though this may not always be the case. Now on to the inner worlds.

In the inner realms the training for Mastership is another thing altogether, and the Soul in training between the levels near the tenth does travel so far and wide that it does experience a myriad of situations and tests that would truly stagger the mind, if its entirety were consciously known. However, most of this training does occur in the dream state and while the shell does slumber, and may not be noticed or experienced by the one who does do it except in dreams or quiet contemplation, when the Master does take the student to other realms and places to study and learn and grow. Often times, this process may be felt as if a train were running through the head of the student when he or she is awake, or as it can be said that the atoms within the bodies can be felt to move at a faster rate as the vibrations of the inner bodies are raised and the impurities and dross are burned in the fiery light of truth and the God-power. Indeed, the range of experience is varied, depending on the Soul, and each will have his experience of doing what it takes to achieve of the great goal. However, within the inner worlds the trials are great and the tests many and do range from battling negative spirits, to wielding of the light, to knowledge of mystical secrets, to techniques and abilities to accomplish certain feats, for each Master does have his or her own area of expertise and specialty, and so, each must attain a basic proficiency and skill to have the initiation of that circle. However, after that basic level is achieved, there is great latitude and flexibility as to what the Soul shall do and what area of interest he hall pursue to succeed in his mission and duties.

The Sugmad, the head of the Grand Sehaji Council, the Lords of Karma and the Silent Nine do collaborate together and view the patterns and actions of man and create the missions and contingencies to keep the universe in balance and all Souls steadily progressing on the path. And so, as each Master does learn and grow and receive of his initiations, specific skills and expertise is learned to fulfill of specific missions that do relate to the conditions and culture and temperament and development of man upon the Earth and those of other places where he does go and serve. For it is important to realize that the universe and all its worlds are constantly evolving and in change, and the changing conditions and circumstances do require of different skills and abilities to effectively do what must be done and lead the man of

39

that time and place on to higher levels of unfoldment and realms of the heavens above.

The Living Sehaji Master is the one who grounds the God-power within the Physical Plane, and for this reason he is granted omniscience and omnipotence to do what must be done in the service of the Sugmad. And so, all other Masters will always defer to the Living Sehaji Master in his will and in his way, for he is the one who brings the light of God to those who need it most and have the most to learn. However, the Living Sehaji Master, who is wise and seeks to find success in his mission and his purpose, does well to consult of those before him as to what they did and learned that can be applied to his mission and time and the challenges he does face, though not all do avail themselves well of this opportunity and wealth of wisdom and experience. And so, the Living Sehaji Master is the Godman who walks within the Physical Plane, and his is the word and law, and all do obey his commands and wishes for the time that he is here and carrying out his duties and responsibilities.

The true aspirant on the path to God, whether in The Way of Truth or any other way, should carefully evaluate of the one who claims to be able to teach and guide and show the way, for many do make the claim of being a Master, and many are false who make the promise of being able to lead a Soul home to God. The student should look for real, tangible, believable proof that satisfies his own curiosity that the Master is able to connect the student to the Light and Sound of God.

But how then may this act be discerned and known? It may take time to properly evaluate of the proof of one who makes these claims, and it is partially for this reason that students in The Way of Truth are required to study for two years before they are given the second initiation and fully connected to the Light and Sound of God, for in the intervening period, the Master does have the responsibility, through act and deed and word, to prove that he is a Master of the path and do what he does say. This may be by showing the student how to use the Holy Spirit to resolve of problems or challenges, or it may include the Master appearing to the student in the dream state or contemplation, or it may include other subtle evidence of change that the student may observe after first connecting to the Holy Spirit with the beginning of the discourses. But in any case, the student should not blindly accept the claims of the Living Sehaji Master or any other without first seeking the proof that shall satisfy his own heart.

Once one is found who you do believe to be a Master of the path that you do follow, then the final test must be to connect the student to the Light and Sound of God, that wisdom and experience might be gained and greater understanding, love and power achieved to aid the student in his daily living, and on the path back home to God. For the true purpose and function of a Master is to bring the student under the cloak of his or her protection and then teach him of the laws and rules and processes, which govern the true existence and nature of the physical and inner planes and begin the student on the road to complete and total Mastery of all that he does experience and sees and knows and encounters in this universe of the Sugmad.

The difference between the Living Sehaji Master and Masters of other hierarchies and traditions is this: the Living Sehaji Master is the one, though not the only one, who is best able to lead many Souls back home to God and to escape forever the wheel of reincarnation. However, this is a point that requires some clarification. There are other existing Masters who are able to help their students forever escape the Wheel of 84. They are few, and they do not have large numbers of students, but they do exist. The uniqueness and special gift of the Living Sehaji Master and the path of The Way of Truth are the great protection they do afford to those upon the path, the speed with which the student may progress and the heights to which the student may ascend while under the protection of this Master, for the Sehaji are a broad and strong brotherhood of Souls who have been created and selected for this purpose and this function, and it is the design of this universe that The Way of Truth shall be the safest, fastest, truest, highest path, which shall exist to return all Souls home to God. So although there are other Souls of merit as Masters of other ways who can help their students escape the Wheel of 84, there are none as powerful or as pure as the Living Sehaji Master who can do what he is able to do, to protect his students and give them grace and return them to the highest heavens above.

The Living Sehaji Master is the purest channel for the highest, most powerful light and love of God in this universe. When a Sehaji Master accepts the Rod of Power or receives the initiation of the tenth circle or above, a permanent connection is created between that Soul and the Ocean of Love and Mercy that is the source of all power, truth, and wisdom within this universe. When that Soul is connected to the power and becomes a conduit for its flow, then any place he does choose to put his attention and direct the flow of light does create such a radiance and purity and goodness that no negativity may remain or contaminate its presence. And so, when a student is initiated by a Master, he is consenting that the love of the Master shall be placed over him to protect him from darkness and the forces of the negative realms. And so, the student does become connected to the Master by a cord of golden light, and as long as the spiritual exercises are practiced and the loyalty to the Master is maintained, then anywhere the student travels within the planes of this universe, the signature and protection of the Master is seen by all and the student is protected from harm.

Also, in this way, if the student should ever find himself in a difficult situation, then he may call upon the Master's love and protection by softly repeating his name or the sacred HU, and this shall activate the cord of connection between the student and the Master and bring the protection that is sought and requested. This is not to say, however, that the student is protected from any karma he must pay, or that if the student does violate of divine law, then there shall not be repercussions to face, for though the Master does give to his students the protection he can offer, the student does still possess free will and the Master cannot interfere in this or any actions or repercussions that do arise from wrong actions that are taken.

So what then does the Master's light truly protect you from? It does protect you from unseen forces that would prey on you and seek to do you harm and from dark angels of the inner realms that do seek to connect with you and cause you distress or negative experiences. Also shall the Master's protection serve to temper and ameliorate the strong negative effects of karma or actions taken, so that the payment that must be made is in an amount and level and pace that is manageable and possible to maintain. Also, too, can the Master's presence protect you from harm from others or from accidents or acts of fate, and the list does go on and on of examples of ways and means in which the Master does seek to keep you safe from harm and injury, so that you may quickly learn the lessons that must be experienced to safely move on to other realms.

The Sehaji Masters truly do love and serve all the students who come to them and many personal sacrifices are made in the name of service and love. The Sehaji Master does give himself wholly to, and joins with, the will of the Holy Spirit; and so, in one sense, his will and desires no longer become his own and he does go as Spirit directs him to serve as he is needed. So his personal preferences for living location, for dress, for travel, for vacation, for reading, even for love can be influenced or directed by the Holy Spirit, if he is to truly serve in the highest capacity he is able. This is not to say that he will become unhappy or despondent, for the force and flow of love experienced by a Sehaji Master is such that may barely be conceived and the honor and joy at serving, thus does make any sacrifice seem a trifling by comparison. But that is not to say that there are no frustrating or lonely times, for this is often the case, especially in personal relationships, for there are few who are able and compatible to spend great amounts of time and be personally involved with one such as a Living Sehaji Master.

And so, the inconveniences and sacrifices are a long list, for the body, as well, does pay a tremendous price to be able to handle the flow of God-power, and sickness and discomfort can result, as the adjustments are made and the body is purified and cleansed to be an appropriate vessel. So do not look with envy at the Master who comes to serve, for it is only out of great love for all Souls below that any Master does leave the comfort and ease of living of the heavens up above and comes to Earth, or any other planet, to endure the discomforts and inconveniences of the physical shell, for that is the only reason that any truly comes to serve the will and love of God.

The Living Sehaji Master can be recognized in several ways; first, by his eyes and the power they do possess when looked upon them deeply; second, by the feeling of love and warmth and power when in the Master's presence; third, by the facility and knowledge and wisdom that is possessed of things unseen or known that could only be considered by one with infinite knowledge and power and understanding; fourth, by the books and teachings he does write to spread the word of truth and the teachings of his heart; and fifth, by the ability to appear to the students in dreams or contemplation and lead the student from his shell to travel and study at the Temples of Golden Wisdom or other places within the inner realms above. And these are a few of the ways that the student's head and heart can recognize a Living Sehaji Master.

When a student's present teacher does pass on to other realms or is replaced by another, then little is seen or known by the student of what does take place in the transfer within the inner realms. The Living Sehaji Master has the mantle of consciousness that may only be borne by one who lives and walks in the Physical Plane. Though there may be more than one Master living, only one does bear the mantle as the conduit and grounding presence and authority for the Holy Spirit upon the Earth. And it is from this mantle that the power of initiation and protection and authority is given and granted to the students, for other Living Sehaji Masters may walk and teach and live at the same time within the Physical Plane, but they shall utilize of the Living Sehaji Master's mantle and only with his consent shall they conduct initiations or bestow upon the students protection, as it does flow from the One. And so, the student may continue to see and call to his former teacher or the one he did begin with. However, that teacher shall now channel his protection and power from the one who bears the mantle and title of the one true Living Sehaji Master on Earth. The student does also have the right and opportunity to now call to the new One, and it shall be as though nothing at all had changed except that a new face and name may now be used to call forth the love and protection that previously had been given by the One that came before.

And so, it should not be a traumatic thing when the Living Sehaji Master does change, for what is important is the mantle of the consciousness and not the personality or the face of the One who wields its force. And so, the student must remember and remain focused on the fact that the universe is in a constant state of flux and change, and especially in The Way of Truth, the moment that things do begin to become settled and crystallized and stagnant, then the dynamic nature of the Holy Spirit does become active and bring change forth once again to keep the teachings vital and new and current to the age and time that needs them most. And so, do Masters and teachers come and go as the universe does ebb and flow and the will of Spirit and the Sugmad does ever adapt to changing times.

The brotherhood of the Sehaji does have of its own mission and purpose and deeds that must be done in service of the Sugmad. However, it is also its sworn duty to serve the Living Sehaji Master in whatever capacity it is able. And so, many do have missions that are directly aligned with his to serve of man on Earth or of different races or peoples on different planets, for not all of the Sehaji or those whom they serve are held in human faces and shells. And so, each of the Sehaji does have specific duties and expertise that have been gained in his many lifetimes on Earth, or one of the other planets within this universe, and in the inner realms, as he has learned and developed and unfolded in his own way and manner.

And so, when each new Living Sehaji Master does come to take his mantle, he will convene of the Grand Council and all will evaluate of his coming mission and what are the likely contingencies to be faced upon this time and period of Earth. And in this analysis and evaluation the necessary skills and abilities will be seen and members of the Sehaji shall volunteer or be asked to serve in different capacities and places to aid of what must be done. In some cases there are those, such as Fubbi Quantz, who have served the same role for many years and little do they change or go to other areas. Others who are more hidden and unseen may come to serve for a specific reason or need that is relevant to the conditions during which the Living Sehaji Master does serve.

So the Master shall, with the agreement of the Council, assemble about him those whom he does wish to have near to aid him in his teaching and management of the universe, when he does embark on his mission, for though he is capable of doing all that needs to be done, if that were the need and requirement, he does have the wisdom and humility to realize that there are those who specialize in certain areas of wisdom and application, and by his observance of the law of economy he does know that it is best for him to call to those who possess the skills to accomplish what must be done in the most efficient manner possible. And so, in this way do all the brotherhood of the Sehaji come and assist the Living Sehaji Master in his will and in his ways.

The Silent Nine are the hidden quiet Masters who are responsible for the efficient functioning of this universe. They do serve of the Sugmad and reside in a quiet temple hidden within the thirteenth plane, though they are always in constant travel and toil to do all that is required to keep the universe in balance and progressing onward toward the goal. They are trained by higher Masters who do possess of great wisdom that has been earned on planes high above any within this universe, and those Masters and teachers do come from and instruct of desirous students in schools beyond this universe of the Sugmad. And so, one who seeks to become and serve as a Silent One must first achieve Mastery in the Order of the Sehaji or the equivalent from one of the other universes of the brothers of the Sugmad and then beseech of admission and acceptance by one of the few great Masters who teaches them the skills and arts of running entire universes, for this is a skill that requires great and difficult training in the esoteric arts and is not a thing to be taken lightly when so many lives and Souls are at stake within even one universe of the Sugmad. And so, the training would commence in a temple on the 20th plane of the heavens and would continue with the skills that are required.

The time does vary in how long it would take, though this is not a relevant conception, for no such thing does exist within the realms of beingness above the Great Divide, but in human terms it might take as little as 5,000 years or as long as 1 million, depending on the Soul in question and how much experience and wisdom is already possessed and how quickly one does wish to progress upon the path. And so, after a time of learning and being tested, one would be ready for assignment in one of the universes of God.

And so, one would go and join the Order of the Silent Nine as a junior member of lower rank and standing to begin his service there. As experience and proficiency does grow and others do leave for other duties, the one would rise in rank and merit within the Order and the universe that he does serve, until at last he would be the head of the Silent Nine for that universe and would have Mastered of all that is to be known and done and would eventually move on to other duties as the mission and cycle of its service did come to an end and close. And so, any who do wish to serve in this capacity should focus on the goal and be unwavering in their dedication and study of the hidden secret arts, for it is a noble calling and one to which few attain, but the universes of God are always expanding and a demand is always seen for those proficient in this art and skill.

The dual nature of the Living Sehaji Master, as an Inner and Outer Teacher, does bring to the student many benefits that others do not have. The most important is the fact that the Living Sehaji Master is able to ground the God energy here in the Physical Plane and in this manner can more efficiently and powerfully distribute it to those who follow him, for although other ascended Masters may be able to communicate their teachings or protect those within the inner realms, it is a greatly superior benefit to have both qualities in the one who leads the way. And so, too, is the Living Sehaji Master able to constantly update the teachings and add to the truth and wisdom that is shared and given freely to the ones who know his name, for the universe is ever expanding and truth does grow and expand to occupy and accommodate the growing layers and planes of wisdom and complexity that do form as the universe evolves and unfolds.

For the universe, too, does have a consciousness that is growing and unfolding as a direct effect of the growing and unfolding consciousnesses of all those Souls who dwell within its realms. And so, the Living Sehaji Master does do of many things, but a great benefit that is given is his constant presence and protection and leadership in a continuity of experience and smooth progression of unfoldment within both the inner and outer planes of the universe.

The Living Sehaji Master is able to stay with the student, while in the physical shell and while traveling into the inner worlds, and this continuity of experience and presence does greatly accelerate the student's progress because there is no gap or waiting or loss of direction and understanding that may occur in other paths, when one component or the other may be missing. And so, the Living Sehaji Master is able to accelerate the experience and learning of the student and burn greater amounts of karma and teach greater amounts of wisdom in a shorter period of time than is possible in other paths and traditions. And these are but a few of the benefits of having an Inner and Outer Master as one and the same person while traveling on the path.

The Living Sehaji Master is one who has perfect love for all life and all living things. But what does this really mean? It means that the Master recognizes the sanctity and sacredness and struggle of all Souls at all levels on the path and in their striving to return back home to God. And the Master does honor each in the way that he does struggle to survive and progress and gain the next higher level of understanding and experience that will take him one step farther on the path. And so, the Master, in his duty, does extend the power and protection and assistance of his love and wisdom to any who is willing to accept it to aid him in his way, and in this manner may the Master be said to honor and love all life and serve it however he is able in the role that he does play.

The Living Sehaji Master and the Sugmad can and do communicate in many ways. First is by direct intuition and heart-to-heart transmission of information or instruction that must be said and done, or the Master may go in contemplation and speak to an embodiment of the consciousness of the Sugmad, or he may speak to one of the Sugmad's emissaries of the Nine or some other who comes to serve Its will and ways, for the Living Sehaji Master does consult of the Sugmad on all-important matters to seek the Sugmad's direction and advice and wishes of what may be done to further Its mission and the unfoldment of man and all others within Its planes. And in this manner does the Sugmad give to the Master additional information he may not have or be aware of, and any instruction or guidance or advice that should be shared to aid of best-laid plans and the service of all in question. And in this fashion it is a relationship of mutual respect and understanding and love in which both do strive together to do what is seen as best for all Souls involved in the many levels and planes and worlds of its universe.

When the Rod of Power is transferred to the new Living Sehaji Master, a temporary stasis is placed on all significant activity within the universe, while all Masters and hierarchies and planes are readjusted and realigned for the next phase of unfoldment and the new direction and cycle that the universe must take, for the Rod of Power is the highest mantle of authority and power within this universe of the Sugmad, and the one who wields it must be known and seen, and must coordinate the efforts of all others, to ensure that the progression and development of all Souls is well kept on track and in balance within all the planes of life and existence.

And so, for a brief instant all does temporarily stay in its place, as the Rod is transferred and all duties reassigned or realigned, as necessary to begin the next phase and cycle of unfoldment in the never-ending journey of Souls upon the path. However, this is not a thing that is even noticed, for the neutral power of sustenance does momentarily come in and keep all in its proper place and balance, while all adjustments are made. And so, no thing or Soul or person is ever even aware of what truly has transpired, save those whose roles have changed and who do work directly with the Master or the Nine of the Sugmad to do what must be done and keep this universe in balance and operation in the manner that must be done and shared to keep all good things in order.

The darshan of the Master is a moment of grace, when the Master connects his heart to the student's, and the student does receive a gift of the pure God-power that the Master is a conduit for. And this gift of love and light creates within the student's heart a feeling of joy and happiness that may last for a moment or a day or a week, depending on the case. And the burst of love and light does also bring to the student the cleansing of impurities and

49

darkness that does dwell within the subtle bodies and in this small measure bring him a small step closer to God, and a taste of the love that does await, when he does finally achieve the wisdom and power and understanding of the initiations of the pure God worlds.

And so, though it is not necessary to be in the Master's presence or sight, this is usually the way the darshan is given, for it is an easier and stronger connection to make, when the Master can see the one he does give his gift to, and also, it is easier for the Master to judge the strength and ability of the student to receive the inflow of love and power, if the student is standing or seated before the Master's gaze. And so, the darshan is given through the word or gaze or touch which does symbolize the act of the heart-to-heart connection that does transfer the light and power and love from the Master to the student.

The number of Sehaji Masters living and walking and working within the Physical Plane at any given time is determined by the conditions on the planet and the mission that is faced by the Living Sehaji Master who does wield the mantle of the power and to which all others do turn to receive instructions and guidance as to what assistance is needed to aid him in his way and with his mission. Now is a critical time, and great imbalance exists between the dark and light; and so, there are several Sehaji Masters present and incarnated in physical shells to aid the Living Sehaji Master, for they carry unquestionable humility and loyalty to his cause. The mission of the Living Sehaji Master determines the assistance he shall receive, and in times of relative balance or slower periods of unfoldment a single Master may suffice to accomplish what must be done.

But this is the time when a new age of man does arise and conditions are thus that several of the Order are needed to keep all balance met and move the consciousness of man and the planet and the universe to the place where it must be to succeed in perfect unfoldment and progress along the plans that have been laid. And so, the Living Sehaji Master will coordinate the efforts and activities of the others to achieve his objectives and desires, both via inner communication and outer, depending on the situation and case and whether the Master is publicly recognized and known for the merit he or she does possess, and in this way, all efforts are made and objectives achieved to succeed with best-laid plans.

The eighth level of initiation is the circle that does begin the probationary period of preparation for Mastership, and the probationary period continues through the eleventh. For each student at and above this level, there is always a primary teacher of the Sehaji who is responsible for the progress and initiations that are taken in contemplation with each succeeding test and level passed. And so, though the Master may change from time to time and based on the occasion and the lessons that must be learned, always there is one who can be turned to for advice and guidance and suggestions of ways to succeed along the path.

The eighth circle does present of many challenges, as do all others in their turn, but the significant one of this circle is to learn to wield the beginnings of the God-power and to remain grounded and balanced, as this new energy does flood the inner bodies and adapt to its new shell, for this is a power of purity and substance unlike any other the student has ever known, and it does take some time and patience and strength to adapt to the new flow and energy of the power from above.

The challenge of the ninth circle is to begin to learn how to use the power with balance and judiciousness and wisdom, and the tests of this plane do involve many situations, which do arise that test the student's patience and judgment and wisdom in the actions he does take to earn the right to stand as a member of the Sehaji and assume his responsibilities in the service of the Sugmad. The ninth circle does take much time to Master and finally to achieve the next level, for once Mastery is conferred, it is a very difficult thing to close down what has been opened; and so, there must be no doubt of the wisdom and readiness of the student to enter into the company of the many of the tenth circle and above. And so, after much training and many trials and tests, the tenth circle is finally conferred and the student is now well on his or her way to becoming a Master and member of the Sehaji, though there still is much to learn.

Once Mastery has been attained, this is only the beginning of the teaching that must occur for the new Master to understand his or her powers and how they may be used and under what circumstances and conditions and what is to be the way and manner and area in which the one does desire to serve the needs of the Order and the wishes of the Sugmad. And so, the tenth circle is spent as a new Master gaining familiarity with the new worlds and expectations and protocols and duties and language and responsibilities of those others of the circle that the one is now a member.

The eleventh circle is the circle when the one has begun to travel and learn and be introduced to the other hierarchies and Souls that do govern them and of the different secret parts of the universe and the many planes and temples and cities that are contained therein and to get his bearing and stature and experience walking among the many to whom he does administer his love and teaching and understanding. This initiatory circle is still probationary. And the eleventh circle is where many do stay for a very long time, as they do the work of the brotherhood and learn the many secrets and things that are necessary to succeed in the many missions and deeds to which all are called upon each day.

And so, after great time and much experience, the twelfth circle is finally achieved and can still be a probationary period for some members of the brotherhood. The true full status as a recognized member of the Sehaji is granted and attendance at Council and in the Order's ways and organization is granted to partake of the many decisions that do govern the universe of the Sugmad, for few are there indeed who do finally earn the thirteenth circle and this initiation of merit and recognition. The members of the thirteenth circle directly conduct the affairs of the Nine and the Sugmad and are the senior council that governs of the Sehaji and all the other Hierarchies within the many planes that are necessary for the efficient functioning of the universe. Also here does the training and selection begin for the Living Sehaji Mastership, and this is a long and arduous process, which few do undertake, and fewer still do succeed in its completion. The Living Sehaji Mastership and the fourteenth circle is the greatest level of wisdom, truth and power which has never been attained in this universe prior to that of the present Living Sehaji Master. The fabric of the God worlds has been expanded to the seventeenth plane to accommodate the balance needed by Sugmad and best-laid plans. And so, the circle of the twelfth, in addition to the administrative responsibilities and day-to-day affairs, does also include ongoing and rigorous tests. The students in Sehaji status can still fall into spiritual slumber, if they fall out of alignment with the Living Sehaji Master's instructions.

The fourteenth plane is reserved for those few who are temporarily taken there for special training by Sugmad, the Nine, the Living Sehaji Master or Milarepa, the head of the Grand Council, for specific tests and training for those few who are finally selected as possible candidates to bear the Living Sehaji Master's mantle. No Soul is given permanent initiation into the fifteenth circle save the Living Sehaji Master, for the time he does wield the Rod of Power, for it is a dual initiation, which includes the fourteenth and the fifteenth together as a unit of initiation to bear the Living Sehaji Master role. And so, the fourteenth is a temporary initiation granted to all others to do what must be done to prepare for the ultimate goal. It will seldom occur, if any Living Sehaji Masters will exceed the fifteenth plane. The seventeenth plane expanded by the Silent Nine, the Grand Council and Dan Rin will house the consciousness of only a few Living Masters in eons to come.

The sixteenth circle is that of the Living Sehaji Master, and there is not always one present on the Physical Plane of Earth, although the mantle is always born and wielded by one in planes above, for if there was not one of this circle, a vacuum would be created and the universe would collapse and all would quickly come to an end. And so, this circle and the fourteenth is always held by one, though he may not have a physical shell, except in times of emergency or great imbalance and unrest within all the planes of this universe.

These are all of the initiations from the eighth to the fifteenth, and though the differences do sound significant, there is in reality a blurred distinction between one level and the next, for the fineness of the vibration and power between these higher realms is nearly indiscernible, except to practiced eyes and ones who are most sensitive to tell.

Although it is true that Soul itself is both male and female combined in the unity of opposites, most Souls, as they do progress well along the path, do eventually adopt a preference for one or the other sex, and this is the characteristic they do bear within the inner realms. Generally, this selection does occur after Self-Realization has been attained and it may change or be abandoned depending on the occasion. Historically on Earth and in this universe, there has been among the Masters a preference for the male aspect. However, as ages change and things do move and continue on in cycles, this too will begin to shift and change and a return to the feminine shall start to be seen. But when Souls are seen and truly act within the inner realms, it is often as the sex they select and has come to be their preference.

There has traditionally been a predisposition to Mastership being sought and conferred by those of the male identification, though this is slowly changing place. For the past many thousands of years, it was a time when the male power was in rising dominance within the Physical Plane, and as an adjunct to the development of the mental body and the manner in which these two streams of energy do work with one another and interrelate. And for this reason, it was necessary that the male aspect predominate the lower realms and take a leading face. And so, many of the highly gifted and talented female Masters have kept a lower profile and operated behind the scenes to allow the development and unfoldment of man to occur, as was necessary and designed within the scheme of best-laid plans. But with the closing of the Age of the Mind and the opening of the age of Soul and of the wisdom of the heart, the female aspect is again ascending to its proper place of merit and balance, and the many female Masters shall begin to come about and be seen and better known for the duties they have done and the many skills and gifts they do posses in equal measure to their brothers who have received so much attention and focus for the last many thousand years.

Traditionally, it has been said that a female could not assume the mantle of the Living Sehaji Master, and in the past this may have been the case, but times do change and traditions and conditions that once dictated the way and workings of the heavens must change, as well and grow. And so, in the future, there may be a woman Living Sehaji Master to lead the flock of the Holy Spirit. The predominant challenge for a woman to wield the Rod of Power and be the Living Sehaji Master here on Earth would be to learn to wield the positive stream of power, which traditionally is better suited and more compatible with the male aspect and form. And so, though it is possible, it shall take a woman of tremendous strength, skill and wisdom to wield the purest power of God within this universe of the Sugmad.

However, there is now an evolution underway and a rebalancing of the universe that has grown too strongly to the right and the male aspect and form. And so, to have a woman Living Sehaji Master would truly be a good thing to balance to the left, which in a few years time the universe would be nearer to the center, which is the place and way that must be maintained, if the ages are to be kept alive and the universe not brought to an end. And so, though there would be many challenges, someday there shall be a woman Living Sehaji Master to lead The Way of Truth and the universe, as it does enter the next great age of man.

After the current Living Sehaji Master, Dan Rin, does relinquish of the body and go on to other realms, there shall be 21 more Living Sehaji Masters before the ages do end and this universe of the Sugmad does sleep and all are put to rest until the great cycle does continue once again. However, it must be understood that the universe is a constantly changing place and though the conditions and possibilities do now present a future with 21 more Living Sehaji Masters, this could truly change, as the free will of man and the evolution of the heavens and of the universe do continue, and all does wax and wane like the tides upon the shore in the ever changing cycle of progression that moves one season to the next as the ages do pass and fade. And so, the time and number of the Living Sehaji Masters is no perfectly certain thing, and the important thing to remember is that there is always one, a member of the Sehaji, that does truly fill that post and always watches over his flock and those within his charge and does take a shell on Earth, when the circumstances do require to aid all noble Souls in the quest and desire to return back home to God.

55

Chapter Four

The Way of the Eternal

"Existence" is the word given to that continuous, infinite state of complete beingness that contains and incorporates, yet does not individually express, the three forces of the universe in a latent, perfect, expressionless whole. It is that state and presence and intelligence which can transcend all the universes below God and even to the very next edge of this known existence. It is what lies beyond God, yet in a realm and way and of a character and essence and fabric that is inconceivable and knowable to few but the most advanced Souls within all these universes of the Sugmad and its brothers, or even the Gods above them. Existence is that thing which transcends beingness. It is the next level of complexity and infinity and sophistication that expands about and above the worlds of beingness in a way that is impossible to describe. For now, what is important to understand is that existence is a vastly more complex state of is-ness, which will someday be explained and known by all Souls within these universes, but not, for a very long time.

On another level, existence within these universes of the ultimate God can be described as that continuous, indestructible, everlasting, infinite state of is-ness that is one of the qualities possessed by Soul. Existence is that characteristic which defines the nature of consciousness; and the endurable consciousness and awareness of Soul, combined with the element of experience that accumulates directionally according to progression, is the definition and explanation of the existent state. For our purposes now, we shall simply know that existence is an essential characteristic of Soul.

Soul is an infinite unit of Sugmad because, if it were not, then, it could be terminable and limited. It must be born and made of the same fabric as life itself for it to possess the abilities to travel and experience and see and know within all the reaches of this universe and others. And so, Souls within this universe were created of Sugmad, as Its sons and daughters, to go and be and form and create the planes and worlds and planets and stars within Its universe. Soul is the same stuff of God, yet not equal to it. It is of the same stuff of the universe, yet a part within it, and not welded or subsumed within it. Soul possesses perspective, awareness, knowledge, understanding and other traits and characteristics that define its nature and purpose. But it must be made of, and exist as, an element of the same stuff as its creator and of the environment in which it exists and experiences, for within the highest realms of this universe, Soul exists by the love from the Sugmad and moves as a point of consciousness within the planes of the Sugmad's heart, and were it to be of the stuff and substance, which were incompatible or dissimilar to the body of its father or its environment, then it would not be able to do all the things for which it was designed and the universe would cease to function as it has been intended and meant. And so, Soul was created as an indestructible piece of the Sugmad's fabric and essence; and so, it does remain and function and mature within the realms and planes of Its universe.

The relationship between the awareness of Soul and Sugmad is a simple one. Sugmad is a sea of Its own consciousness, but because all Souls are pieces of Itself, it can sense and feel and see the collective experiences and impressions and learning and understanding of all within Its universe. For Sugmad, it is very difficult to identify and pinpoint the awareness and experience and understanding of any given individual Soul, unless that Soul is highly developed and powerful and mature. For it is like trying to see the reflection of a single pinhead within a mountain of diamonds. Yet it is a simple thing, with the lessons and learning of the Sugmad, to feel and sense and know the waves and swirls and eddies and rolling trends and motions of the collective consciousnesses of the groups of Souls and planets and solar systems and other aggregations within all the realms of Its universe. And so, since the Soul is a separate and discrete unit of

58

the fabric of Sugmad, it has its own experiences and wisdom and understanding, which is its own and its alone. But because the Soul is comprised of the fabric of Sugmad, of the light and love and sound of existence, its consciousness and awareness, when combined with the infinite other of its brothers and sisters, may be seen and felt and experienced, as well, by the Sugmad in Its home of the Ocean of Love and Mercy on the fifteenth plane above.

The sacred "HU" was conceived and created within this universe to be the key to unlocking the secret power of the ethers by its frequency and vibration, which is unique and all its own. This universe of the Sugmad is unique and different from any other in its energetic signature and frequency that is the mark of Sugmad's heart. And so, because of the uniqueness of its patterns and elemental energies and range of frequencies of vibration, the HU is the word that is keyed to specifically unlock and access the hidden power of the heart of love and wisdom and understanding within this universe. Within another universe, with a different range of energy and characteristics, there would be a different word created to be the key to unlocking of the secrets and power within that universe. And so, it is the gift of the Sehaji and Sugmad to give to all Souls this understanding and this powerful key to aid them in their endeavors and their journeys back home to Its heart and arms above.

As the Soul begins to awaken to its true purpose and nature, its vibration and frequency does begin to rise, and the Soul does need some means of powering this ascension and growth beyond the normal existence it does have. Comparatively, you cannot send a rocket to the moon without a propulsion system; and so, too, cannot Soul find its way to the heavens without a key of power to unleash the fuel of the universe and send it on its way. And so, is the HU given to unlock the hidden secrets and give the Soul the means to accessing the power of God to aid it on its way and in its endeavors.

"Maya," or illusion, was created as a part of the lower universe because there needed to be some way and manner and mechanism for Soul to have to struggle and be tested and mature and learn the lessons and skills and depth of compassion and beingness that was desired to aid the works of creation and existence, for if all Souls were merely born and given the full breadth of their powers and abilities, then the universe would merely be a streaming ball of light without any differentiation or difference or variation. For Souls, by their own use and creativity and ignorance, do create the very Maya that they seek to escape; and so, the system is self-perpetuating and never ending and thus is the full breadth and expression of emotion, creation, experience and learning accomplished and seen and known.

For Maya is the elemental material of learning within the lower worlds below the Great Divide, yet Soul does take the memories of the experiences of what it learned in the fields of illusion below and returns to higher heavens and continues the process of creation, yet in a balanced and perfect state; and so, the lessons of the Maya are not only to help Souls to grow and mature and understand of their own nature and abilities, but also to serve as inspiration and memory for when Souls do rise above the Great Divide and continue in their duties in the planes and hierarchies above.

In the lower worlds, Maya, or the negative force or illusion, does bind to the God-power, or love, to create all that is seen and experienced within the lower five planes of the Sugmad. The key to enjoying and maximizing this experience is to gain the ability and sight to clearly see between the two, for there is nothing wrong with living and experiencing and enjoying the illusions, for they add a richness and depth and breadth to life that makes existence interesting and moving forward within the lower planes. The key and the test are to learn to have the experiences in a balanced manner and detached from their negative power, which is what does bind Souls here and within the lower realms.

The negative power, or illusion, in the lower five is an essential element of the trinity of creation, sustenance and destruction and not something to be feared or to be avoided. However, it must be seen and known and experienced in the proper context and proper manner in the way it was intended and the purpose it does serve. And so, for those advanced students on the path, seek always to determine in any given situation or moment what is the element of love, and what is the element of illusion, and this process of learning discernment is one of the greatest and most difficult skills that must be Mastered within these lower worlds below.

Within the lower five planes of this universe, time and space are seen and experienced because Soul must have a continuity and progression of experience and unfoldment. Time is personal and relational for each Soul and also as a collective experience. A Soul's unfoldment and events and occurrences are to a large extent already known and planned, with the exception of certain contingencies for free will and changes in direction. But, by and large, a Soul has already mapped out its experiences and the path of its journey before it is ever begun, both in terms of this lifetime and in the grander, greater scheme.

And so, time is the experience of moving along the progression, sometimes back, sometimes forward, towards a greater unfoldment and realization of the true nature of the self. And space, as well, is created as the environment in which to place experience such that the perception of this movement is known and understood, and the relationship between events can be properly placed and organized so that confusion and madness does not occur. For example, in the case of that experience commonly known as déjà vu, this occurs when a Soul has an experience in normal space - time, but also is conscious to the memory of the event from when it was planned and experienced already within the inner planes.

And so, within the higher worlds, where the Soul or higher self has the perspective and wisdom to see the broader scope, all things are placed openly in view, and the point where Soul decides to place its consciousness and attention is the point where time exists and the lower selves are activated to have that series of experiences. And this is governed by the rate, pace and development of the Soul's progression towards unfoldment and a higher state of knowledge and awareness. For if Soul had the maturity and wisdom and development to not need the lessons of the lower realms, then time and space would not need to exist and the worlds of duality would cease to function and be created and destroyed.

61

"Reality" is the term given to the experiences had and processed and perceived by each individual Soul. "Society" is the consensual reality of groups of Souls who agree to agree on common experiences or standards as the basis for interaction and trust and cooperation. The difference, in some cases, between saints and madmen is their ability to create a consensual reality around the experiences they have and the worlds they experience and know. And so, reality is sought, experienced and created by each Soul to bring to it the personal experiences it requires to aid it in its way and in its progression, and to teach it the lessons it needs to learn to progress along the path.

And for those Souls who fail to learn the lessons that are presented, that Soul recreates different variations of the same reality scenario until the lesson is learned and the cycle broken and the Soul is ready to move on. And for some Souls, they can become crystallized in their reality circuit, with the same scenarios repeating for even up to 1,000 years or more, depending on the nature of the lesson and the circumstances of Soul and its readiness to move on. Also, a factor is the strength and power of the Soul and its ability to quickly or slowly manifest the situations and environments and reality that is best suited to teach the lessons it needs to learn. And so, this is the nature of reality, for each Soul that walks and breathes, which has created its own experiences, and is responsible for its own place and conditions, to have those lessons which it does know it needs to move on to higher realms.

There exists a vacuum of time-space within which each individual Soul has its experiences, and this can be better described as the reality, which is directly and immediately perceived by the active senses of man in his immediate environment. This is as a personal reality vacuum that surrounds and encompasses each Soul. Now when each of these personal realities collide and interact with those of others, then these spheres of reality develop overlapping sections like two circles drawn with a shared portion between the two. And the aggregation of these shared reality spaces are what create the collective consciousness of man and communities and cities and nations and planets and universes and on and on.

And so, the collective reality and consciousness of a group is a reflection of all those within it and the experiences and conditions they have created to bring the lessons they need collectively to them to progress further on the path. And the special ability and gift of prophets and saviors is the way that they are able to energize and charge the power and vibration of their personal reality sphere to uplift and raise and change the collective consciousness of the whole and bring an entire society or people to a higher level of understanding and awareness. And so, this is the relationship between individual reality and the time-space vacuum and collective consciousness and the unfoldment and progression of Soul.

In the lower worlds and planes of illusion, the Sugmad must express Itself and communicate with those of its emissaries through symbolic acts and metaphors, for the power of Its love and message must be combined with the negative power of Maya or illusion to say what must be said or else all balance would be upset and life and the universe would become undone. For the pure God-power cannot by Itself exist in the lower worlds without causing chaos and disaster. And so, this is why Participants in The Way of Truth are taught of how to see and recognize the Eternal Wisdom of the Masters, when it is spoken or given unknowingly through another, for this is the way the Sugmad and Its emissaries communicate within the lower worlds.

For the mark of a true Master and spiritual adept is the knowledge and ability to do what must be done in a way that is karmically neutral and free of imbalance. And so, when you do witness of certain gurus or psychics or others who appear to have the ability to wield the fabric and power of God to do of miraculous things, this may truly be the case. However, the mark of their true wisdom and development and merit is if they are able to do these things in a way that is compatible with Spirit's goals and does not create any karma or throw the universe out of balance or into disaster.

And so, the key ability and strength of the Living Sehaji Master is not in his showy ways or public spectacles or miracles and acts of grace, though he is capable of doing all these things and more, it is his ability to use the God-power to accomplish his mission and desires in a way that creates no ripple or effect or echo within the karmic waters that keep the Wheel of 84 turning and alive. And so, the Living Sehaji Master will look for ways and opportunities to blend this power with the fields of illusion and Maya; and so, in a subtle way, create the outcomes he does desire, but in a manner that creates no karma for him or any others involved.

This is the essence and truth of living completely in harmony with God and all others, and this is why the Living Sehaji Master is the most highly developed Soul in the universe, because he is able to see and is skilled in the ability to be patient and do what must be done in a manner that serves the highest spiritual good of all and not the selfish interests of himself or the few that follow him. And so, he is trained and does know how to blend his tremendous power with the fields of illusion and Maya, which create the lower worlds and gently nudge and shift all conditions to do his will and ways. And this is why The Way of Truth is considered a higher path, because it does require the subtle skill of discernment to see the gentle twists and turns and gifts that the Living Sehaji Master does give his students to guide them on the path and in their lessons and learning.

The techniques to separate Maya from Truth and come to proper decisions are these:

1. First, call to the Master in quiet contemplation until the mind does rest and you can begin to imagine the blue light. Then see the situation with which you are faced and see it enveloped slowly within the light as it dissolves and fades away. Then, ask the Inner Master to show you the truth of what is real, and in this way you shall receive a thought or image or impression or understanding of what is the truth of the matter. And for those less practiced in the art, you shall receive in a day or several a flash of thought and understanding, which does explain to you the truth you do desire.

2. Go into contemplation and see the Master's light, and then into the light, place the following words: "Master, show me the truth in the area I now see illusion." And in this way shall the Master bring to you the ability to discern the truth of the situation you do face.

Both of these are good techniques to see the truth within the illusion, and may be used by any level of student to aid him on his path and in his endeavors.

Sri Gopal Das (spoken directly and verbatim)

As man does grow and move forward on the path, his reality and perception with the illusions does change and grow according to his abilities. And typically, this progression does occur and is shared in a common fashion amongst many similar Souls who are at the same general place and progressing at the same general pace. And so, as they do each gather experience and learn, their own reality matures and grows and with it the consensual collective reality of all the group of Souls. And so, Spirit does observe this progression, and the Lords of Karma, as well, and the Nine, and then lessons are given accordingly on an individual and collective basis to either accelerate or slow the progression of the group to keep pace with best-laid plans and the unfoldment and mission of the universe.

And so, the individual lessons of illusion are sometimes tied to the level of the collective whole, for if any Soul should progress too far ahead or fall too far behind, without the proper balance, then society would become unstable and he or she should find himself or herself in a precarious and unpredictable position. The exception to this is those Souls who are destined and have agreed to play the role of fracturing of the collective consciousness that a great leap forward or backward should take place according to the plans and desires of the Lords of Karma and the Nine. And in these cases, the individual illusion and Maya of all other Souls within the collective consciousness shall be primed and readied that the message and the teachings of the one should be accepted and realized and great progress and evolution made to move along the path.

In ancient Egypt, when it was my time as the Master upon the Earth, things were much more fluid as does regard the separation between the planes and the ability to project out of the body and explore of other realms. And so, I did teach the secrets of The Way of Truth within the temples of those lands, and it was my Order of

65

monks and adepts who built the pyramids of stone and aided the Pharaohs in their conquests and great deeds of merit and wonder. And since this was a time of less developed mental powers and abilities, the strength of the illusions was easier to see and perceive for the truth that lay behind.

And so, under the guidance of my hand and others of my teachers, the Holy Spirit was given in a high, pure state and free of all the illusions to many who were of our number and studied in our ways. However, this was also to be our undoing, for it was the purity of the teachings that created an imbalance; and so, the negativity and illusion did have to begin to come to fill the vacuum created by the light. And in this way was all balance kept and the truth of the teachings shared, that those who were adept did know how to see and could differentiate between the two, yet it was necessary for some of the illusion to come, to have all balance kept.

In the years and centuries that have passed since that time, the teachings of The Way of Truth have gone through many cycles. At some times they were public and robust, at other times hidden and secretive, yet always at some place and by some Master, hidden or otherwise, have the teachings been kept and taught to those who yearned to know.

And now in modern times there is a rebirth of the teachings and the truth and the power contained within, yet the challenges are greater in this age because of the greater strength of the mind and of illusion to keep man from the light.

And so, greater care must be taken to carefully watch and evaluate that the illusion should be well separated from the truth, for a pure path such as The Way of Truth does well attract the darkness of illusion to balance of its light. And so, in those within and surrounding the teachings, one always must be aware and listen to the heart and utilize the skill of discernment to tell what is the truth and what is the illusion that is seen and beside its face, for the two can become closely intertwined and can be confusing for those newly upon the path.

The Way of Truth is the path protected by the Living Sehaji Master, who is the closest Soul to Sugmad of any upon the Earth, and for this reason, he shall always give to his flock the power and love of the highest regions, for this is his home above and his duty and his purpose to bring this love and power to Earth. And so, The Way of Truth is a path that always shall be laden with the love and power of the Sugmad, for this is its heritage and destiny as the path of the Light and Sound and the Order of the Sehaji.

There does come to each student, each day, and every moment, challenges and opportunities to act in different ways, and it is the constant test and lesson to keep true to the golden way and always upon the path. And the best way for the student to be sure that his actions and decisions are true to the Sugmad and the way of the Eternal is, before each action is taken, or before each word is said, to within the imagination, repeat this sacred phrase, "I do this in the name of the Sugmad." And in this fashion will all actions always be checked and taken in the manner that is of highest service to all who are involved for the greatest amount of good, and in this way will the student progress upon the path and quickly find himself at the level where he does desire to be and of the circle to which he does strive.

Chapter Five

The Keys to Greater Understanding

Leytor (spoken directly and verbatim)

The keys to understanding all that is seen and experienced about the student in his reality in each day and moment in time are the five different techniques which do enable the student to separate illusion from reality and truth and see into the heart of what really is the matter and root cause of all that does affect him.

The first technique and key is this, to softly sing the HU in the imagination, in a quiet place, while the situation is pondered and the answer truly sought with an open heart and desire to know the proper course.

Second, to quietly ask for the Master whenever a situation does arise where the truth and proper action is difficult to discern and then watch for a subtle sign or key, as to the proper way and method to do what should be done.

Third, to see the words written in the imagination that describe the situation or question that one is faced with and concerned where you wish to find a deeper understanding and perspective of what is the truth and way, and after the words are written on the inner eye to see, the answer will be forthcoming in the hours or days to come.

Fourth, to ask the question while visualizing the Master and giving to his heart, the words of question and perplexity, which you do wish to see and understand, and know the proper course.

And fifth, and the most powerful technique for understanding is, in quiet contemplation, to go and place the entire situation within the blue light of pure love and God-power and ask to truly be shown the truth, as it may be and does exist in this time and situation with regard to the question you do have and wish to understand. And by using of these five keys and ways to understanding, the student shall never find himself perplexed or confused as to what is the truth or meaning or proper course to take when faced with the illusions or the other negative fields which do confound one's life.

In the daily life of the student there are situations and challenges with which he is faced with each day and moment where the proper course of action or understanding may not always be clear. And so, the key to right and proper action is to know what truly are the cause and root energy and karmic implication of each and every challenge that is faced upon the path. And so, the seeker does gain in the ability to recognize and see the situations and conditions which are brought to him each day as opportunities and tests of what is the proper way and action to do what must be done. Then, having and using these techniques is a simple, efficient way to better life and living and always moving on and progressing on the path back to the Sugmad's heart.

When understanding of each and every situation is gained and learned to see, then truth is always apparent and illusion begins to lose the hold upon your heart and of your actions. And as greater amounts of truth are recognized and known and acted in a proper situation, then greater amounts of love and light are channeled through the higher self and into the lower bodies of man and woman to burn away the dross and raise of the vibration and speed the progress of the seeker on his way back home to God. And so, in this manner are the inner bodies cleared more efficiently and quickly and the student does soon find that his outer initiations are accelerating with the pace of his unfoldment and the clearer eyes he has to see the truth of what is all about him in the daily challenges he faces.

With these secret keys and techniques, the student does learn to clearly see that everything in his reality is a lesson and opportunity to gain a higher degree of truth and understanding of the hidden ways of God and secrets of his heart. For all reality is truth and love blended with negativity and illusion, and to separate the one from the other and see all for what it is, is the gift from the Living Sehaji Master, to clear away the obstructions and live a better life of clearer decisions and opportunities to grow and always move on. And so, everything the student does see or experience becomes spiritualized and polarized to clearly provide the truths and lessons Soul does seek to progress along the path.

When these keys are Mastered and put into daily practice and use with steady discipline, then the inner bodies do begin to receive of more light and power and love and gradually all dross and impurities are burned away and all that does remain is the pure stuff of Soul and the student is well on the way to Self-Realization and God-Realization, for to finally find these states is to know and always see the truth in each situation and the cause of each and every act that does come to face each day the one who walks upon the Earth and carries of the mission and duty of service to the will of the Sugmad, to be a vessel and a channel for the love It seeks to give and share to all Its children below. And so, for those who are willing and have the discipline and the ability, this is truly a good way to quickly and efficiently, move rapidly on the path to the higher planes above.

The mind and heart are the two opposing forces that create the illusion and tension and balance that comprise the lower worlds. The mind fabricates illusion, the heart; truth. And so, man's great challenge in this next age is to quiet the raucous mind and allow it to quietly rest and to open the heart to hearing and perceiving the truth and love of higher realms that Soul does wish to say to it.

The mind does perceive of life as an illusion to be won at higher and higher levels with no end or final destination in sight, only that for each new level gained, whether in financial achievement, sports, homes, jobs, educational degrees, cars, clothes, wives or whatever is the case, the mind does always seek a greater level of gratification and pleasure and accomplishment and does tell the lower self that only if this next level can be achieved shall true happiness and pleasure be finally known and realized. And this is the great paradox of the illusion, for it is a game that never can be won.

The heart, in contrast, does seek of truth, which requires nothing of material illusion, save the basic requirements for sustenance and simple comfort to keep Soul's shell happily and safely maintained at a level that allows the undertaking of quiet contemplation and a basic life of comfort and safety. This is not to say, however, that men of God must be poor or hermits or cannot enjoy the many pleasures of life and successful living, for this is truly not the case. However, those finer and more pleasurable things of a material existence must be garnered and won in a karmically neutral fashion and without attachment or due fixation on the end that is finally achieved, for a man or woman of God does learn and know how to create the life that is desired in harmony with Spirit and God's laws, and this is the key to having all that you desire, but in a way that does not violate the purpose and nature of Soul's existence on this plane.

And so, for the mind, the purpose of compassion is a thing that is to be done to achieve of material gain as well by impressing friends or upholding moral conventions of the social consciousness that exists and enslaves the actions and ways of the mental body of man. Whereas the heart does view compassion as an act of grace and truth, by seeing the root cause and energy of each action in each situation and acting in the manner that honors the position and challenge and intention that the Soul in question does take along its own path, of its learning and unfoldment.

Of wisdom, the mind does view as just experience gained through living that allows the mind to make more advantageous decisions to gain the goals of illusion it seeks with greater haste and efficiency. The heart, however, does view wisdom as the accumulated understanding of the higher law of God and the increased facility of living and walking and acting in Its will and in Its way in a manner that is karmically neutral and supports the highest interest of all the Souls involved.

And finally of love, the mind does view in purely practical terms as an extension of the need to procreate and the physical desires of

72

the hormonal body and merely nothing more of a higher level or understanding; whereas, the heart does know that love is a many leveled connection between two Souls who wish to support each other and express their divinity within the physical world and become together a channel for the greater love and power of God to those who need it most.

Of friends and family and God, the mind does view them in haphazard order, with no Hierarchy of merit or wisdom, but only in the order and direction that in that moment best serves of his desires and intentions to further his own cause. Yet for the man who lives with his heart, he does arrange his loyalty and devotion in the progression from first, God, then family and then friends as a hierarchy of importance and priority of service and of love.

And so, there are many differences between the ways in which the heart and mind do differ in their understanding and desires and have created the reality upon the Physical Plane on Earth and in the other realms and regions of the lower five Planes of God. And it is the intent and purpose of this next great age of man that more love and understanding and truth should now begin to come in and balance of the negative mental power that has dominated Earth for the last 2,000 years and created the challenges and problems that do exist today in such imbalance and poor proportion.

True forgiveness is one of the keys to ascension and spiritual achievement within these lower planes. To truly forgive means that Soul is able to have compassion and see behind the action to the true reason and root energy of the illusion or fear or other cause that did lead that Soul to transgress against you in a manner you did find unpleasant or unjust, for each Soul, in its essence, is only love, and any violation of Divine Law or your free will is done only out of ignorance of the proper ways and means of conduct according to the higher self, and it is the challenge and the lesson of each Soul here on Earth to learn the proper way and means of acting in accordance with Divine Law.

And so, true forgiveness is the ability to see the way that each Soul does err in its judgment with the actions it does take and for you to open your heart to that Soul and send it true love and compassion, with no trace of fear or malice or hate, and truly and honestly wish it the best fortune and greater wisdom to aid it on its path. And in this way are all karmic patterns and engrams between you both erased, and you have created a neutral relationship with detached love and goodwill as its basis, which is the way and manner that shall ultimately set you free of the Wheel of 84 and return you to your home above.

In life on Earth, we live in a dual state of experience combined of both the negative and the positive. It is the fabric and essence of what comprises the lower worlds. And to exist in this state, in balance, then one must experience both sides of the energetic spectrum to keep balance in the lower bodies until the connection to the higher self may be opened and the pure power of love and beingness brought into the lower selves. Even then, these dual emotions and experiences still exist but are now viewed with a detached perspective; and so, the immediacy and the range of fluctuation is less and the perception of the experience is diminished, although the conditions which provoked and created it are the same as they were before.

And so, these ranges of human experiences in life - joy and disappointment, pleasure and pain, sadness and happiness - may truly be said to be artifacts of the experiences of the ignorant and attached lower selves and not necessary conditions of the circumstances of the experiences themselves. However, these dual experiences do serve a true and useful purpose to aid the seeker in his learning and progression.

A notable experience with any of these states is an indicator that in that area of one's life and lower bodies, there is an attachment or a darkness within the energetic selves that needs to be viewed and cleared, for when the detached state is achieved, then all experience is viewed with understanding and truth, and the illusion and negativity of the unclear eyes is not experienced, except as a perceived and allowed reaction within one of the lower bodies that is under control of the higher self.

And so, when you do find yourself in the midst of any one of those experiences listed above, you should look deeply to the root cause and energy behind the sensations and reactions you are having, for in this way of honest and discerning self-examination, you will quickly find and see the attachments and blind spots and weaknesses you still do have which keep you from progressing into the return to the heart of God. And once a diagnosis of self has been made, then, it is a much more simple matter to seek and find a way to remedy of what you do wish to change.

When others do act upon us in unwanted and painful ways, we must take care to look deeply at the Soul and at the matter to see what is the root cause and energy, for rarely are people honest and true as to what really is their motivation for the things they say and actions they do take, on either side of the equation. And so, to be able to see what really is the energetic seed that has festered and grown to the proportion that an unwanted action has been created, you must look upon the Soul and situation with compassionate, loving eyes and discern the true nature of what has occurred, for rarely is the nature and essence of your true self the cause and reason for the action that is seen.

More typically, these unwanted and unpleasant actions are perceived and seen as the other person does experience in some twisted and misshapen way some fear of his own psyche and lower selves that he does not know how to face or adequately resolve to his own satisfaction and with the level of development and understanding he does himself possess. And so, in each case and instance, you would do best to look with loving eyes at the other person and strive your best to see what the real motivation is, within his own misperception, and fear is the root energy and cause of action he does take.

However, a word of caution must be uttered here. Most Souls are not awake to, and aware of, what causes them to act, and to awaken them to those reasons prematurely may activate a cycle of resolution before it is truly the right time and create a karmic linkage between you and that Soul. The way to resolve of the situation is to see with detached eyes the reason and cause of the action and then to give detached goodwill and love to the person without speaking of the reason or what you do perceive to be the problem at its root. In this way are all negative actions returned and resolved at their point of origin. Thus, you are kept in a neutral position and free of karmic debt and the situation shall be resolved in a more quick and efficient manner.

Forgiveness and an abundance of love are intricately and intimately linked together as two ends of the same piece of twine, though the association and cause is something rarely seen or understood. When one does truly and honestly practice forgiveness to others about him who have wronged him or caused him harm, then he is creating an energetic field of neutrality and love, which surrounds his own being and creates a resonance of vibration that dictates the interaction of all those who come to him.

Dark or negative feelings or thoughts create energetic footholds for others to grab and attach to and pull themselves into your presence and reality. However, an aura of forgiveness and love does create a shield from these types of people and energetic patterns; and so, though they may approach you, they cannot find a hold to sustain themselves in your presence and swiftly must move on. And so, to find yourself surrounded by many who love you truly, practice always the state of detached goodwill and forgiveness and you shall always find that the love you are and send is always returned to you and that those with darkness in their hearts and minds shall flee before your coming and leave you safe from harm.

To truly forgive others who have caused you pain and harm and to let go of the hurt they have created in your life can truly be a difficult matter, however, there are a few techniques to aid you in your cause.

The first is to go in contemplation and call to the Inner Master. Then in his presence, and with the imagined presence of the other, declare to the one who has caused you pain your heartfelt forgiveness and goodwill for the ignorant actions he did take to create the hurt you have felt. Then, imagine the arms and blue light of the Master enveloping you both, as you honestly and deeply repeat this affirmation of forgiveness until the pain and hurt has completely dissipated and gone. Though this may take awhile, the pure light of love from the Master's heart shall aid to burn off any residual negativity and darkness within the inner bodies and the karma that links you both.

Another way to seek and find forgiveness is, when you are in the presence of the one who has hurt you and caused you pain, to in your third eye see the image or blue light of the Master and in your heart repeat, "I forgive you and love you as Soul." And with the true and honest silent repetition of this affirmation, the hardness and negativity of the pain and hurt shall begin to fade and dissolve and the light of love shall be returned, and you shall be freed from the negative vibrations and karma that truly binds you to the other and the Wheel of 84.

Friendship and love is an oft misunderstood and abused notion in modern times and living. True friendship and love is the heartfelt service and devotion to the happiness of another without any desire or objective for the return or gain to yourself, for love is a pure force of being and does not require compensation in any form or way for the act in which is it given. And so, to develop lifelong friendships and loving relationships with those you do have near your heart, then strive always to place yourself in the position and circumstance of the other and see what would be the thing or action that would bring happiness and joy to the other without regard for reward or recognition.

And in this way you will open the door and energetic channel for the pure love and power of God to enter in and remove of any impurities and dross that does interfere in your loving friendship or relationship with another. And too, this practice can become a way of transcendence and good progress toward the higher realms above, as you do purge of the negativity and darkness that can take root within the places in the energetic bodies that do extend and relate to others.

However, it must always be remembered that balance is to be kept and Divine Law observed, for it is easy to become a martyr and to abandon the duty to self in the name of love and service to another. The first duty and imperative of any Soul is to its own preservation and well being, for one cannot be a co-worker and participant with the Sugmad if one is causing oneself harm and degradation in the

77

mistaken thought and act of service to another. And so, this is the test to be passed in relationships and love, of how to truly love and serve another with an open and true heart, while honoring the requirements and needs of your own true self and position within the worlds of God.

There are for each seeker specific energetic and karmic signatures in others that are more compatible and positive with the nature of the self. And so, the challenge and opportunity is to bring into the life those that promote harmony and balance and support the desires and destination of the higher self of Soul. And so, the following technique may be used to bring others into the life with balance and no karmic repercussions.

The technique that you do desire to bring balance to the life and to bring a significant other is this: First, to sit quietly in silent contemplation and repeat the sacred word. Then to imagine the blue light of the Master as it does come to you. Then, imagine your own energetic bodies as an hourglass of liquid gold and energy, and imagine outside that you swim in a sea of the light and love of God. Then, see the Master's hand reach to you, and as he does touch your side, the levels within the glass and the outer sea do balance and become one. This shall bring the balance you do desire. Next to bring a partner into your life, you must see, again, the light and say to the Master, "Bring me one who will add joy and balance to my life and share with me the pleasure of love and companionship." This shall be the way to most quickly put your request into the life force and bring to you with haste the resolution that does serve the highest spiritual good of all involved.

The key issue and point that cannot be stressed enough or given enough attention is this: You cannot find happiness with another before you have found it within yourself. This is a simple law and fact that is the most widely misunderstood and misinterpreted of any other. You create in your reality what you are in your energetic bodies and selves. And so, any unhappiness or darkness that lingers in yourself must necessarily be manifested in the relationships with those about you, for the reality you experience is always a reflection of you.

And so, to find and experience true happiness and love in relationship, you must first be able to find it within yourself, or else it shall remain an impossibility. So the best advice that can be given is to mercilessly and honestly look within at the pain and hurt you suffer, and then seek to resolve these things as matters within yourself and not as the fault and responsibility of any other. And when you have achieved the state of true happiness within yourself, then shall you finally find true happiness with another, for you shall draw to you within your reality and reflection the same as which you are, and you shall then experience in the arms of another the love you radiate from the core and true being of your own self.

The relationships we do experience with all other Souls are of only three types and nature: One, to collect a debt that must be repaid from the other; two, to repay a debt that is owed by you to another; and three, for mutual love and support. However, this situation and truth is further confounded by the fact that relationships do have their own cycles and progression and a relationship may start as one condition and then with time and experience transform into another; and so, the key is always to be aware of what is the dynamic being enacted, to always know the proper course and action to be taken.

The impact this can yield on the relationship we seek to have can be this: If we do wish and desire to guide and develop each relationship into the karmically neutral and beneficial position of mutual love and support, then each interaction and connection must be given and held from that position within your own true heart, for in this way shall debts be paid and others be forgiven and the relationship can progress to the desired state. There is as well, however, another technique which can be utilized to help to speed the progression to the desired end. In contemplation you can go and seek of the Living Sehaji Master. Then in his presence, bring the other and have him or her stand with you within the light of the Master's love. And in this light say and declare, "I have only detached goodwill and love for you, and I offer you payment for any debts owed, and I forgive any owed to me." And with the repetition of this mantra and action over a period of days or weeks, the debt will be more quickly and painlessly paid and resolved without any actual action having to take place in the physical realm, or at least to a reduced degree. And so, in this way can those relationships with others that do have some karmic root that requires resolution be quickly and efficiently dealt with and moved to the position of mutual love and support that always should be sought and desired.

The imagination is a little understood or utilized faculty of man that is the key to all understanding and creation. For the understanding of life, the imagination must be used to develop an awareness of and see the core root energies and causes of all things that the seeker does experience. The understanding of life is driven by the ability to temporarily place oneself in the perspective and state of consciousness of the other and by this manner see the direction behind the action from his own eyes and perspective, even to a greater or deeper degree than he, himself, is able.

It is actually the bi-location of the consciousness into a split perspective, with the one retained in the seeker's own heart and frequency and vibration and the other adapting and melding the consciousness to the frequency pattern and vibration of the other, and this is done through the powerful faculty of the imagination.

So to use the faculty most efficiently, the skill is to feel energetically the pattern of action and energy of the other who acts against you with the facilities of the higher self, then to place the consciousness temporarily there to see what is the cause and reason behind the action of the other, and in this way will the seeker gain the skill and ability to perceive behind the veil of illusion and gain an understanding of the root cause and energy of all that crosses his path.

In a similar manner, the imagination is the key to the attainment of our life goals, for the imagination is the paintbrush used by Soul to create the tapestry of our future life to which we will walk into as we progress through experience and time. And so, the seeker must master this faculty to create the conditions and circumstances that are desired to have the life he wants. The Soul is a powerful body and aspect of the unit of awareness that is the true self, and when in the human physical consciousness it is through the imagination that the lower bodies connect to Soul and hear its heart and share its wishes and desires. And so, Soul takes the information shared and perceived from the lower bodies and creates imagination pictures, or thought forms, and returns them to the lower bodies. And as they descend through the lower bodies, they begin to take on the shape and characteristic and substance, through the different inner planes, that eventually comprise the physical manifestation and expression on Earth. And this does truly apply and hold true for negative and well as positive thought forms and expressions.

It is a frustrating characteristic of the Physical Plane that this process does take more time to accomplish, for in the higher realms above the Great Divide it is an instantaneous process, however, such is the reality of this plane and the lessons it entails. The important rule and fact to remember, however, is that the prolonged and active and disciplined use of the imagination is the key to realization of the goals that are desired.

If it can be imagined and felt as a reality within your heart, it can be achieved if the discipline and focus is had to pursue what is sought. So the key to conscious creation and living is this: When in quiet contemplation and connected to the higher selves, always remember to paint the picture in vivid detail and true feeling of the thing you do desire, and do not waver or falter from your goal, and eventually it shall come to you through the aid of the Holy Spirit.

The Law of Assumption is a basic law of the universe that can be utilized to obtain the goals we seek. It is a corollary and extension of the principle of the imagination. The Law of Assumption states that we will become and realize what we assume ourselves to already be. However, this does require some explanation. It is not the same as assuming the situation is already presently manifested, for this would lead to bizarre actions and contradictory expression of consensual reality were every person to walk about acting and talking and proceeding as though he were within a reality which was out of synch with all of those around him.

The Law of Assumption is this. Place yourself in the conscious, feeling state where it is assumed and known and understood that that which you seek is already agreed to as an element and part of manifested physical reality and that it is moving through the planes and process of manifestation toward you, that you may soon step into and find yourself living in that place where you desire to be, and thus by living always in the state of assumed expectation of imminent fulfillment, you polarize and energize the energetic bodies to create a resonance that attracts and opens you to those things you have desired and created in your imagination and through the imaginative techniques. And in this way are dreams and wishes realized in an efficient and expeditious manner.

To use this technique to attain and prioritize goals such that all things are achieved with the blessing of Spirit and in accordance with Divine Law and karmically neutral action, this is the way to proceed. When in quiet contemplation, see the image and scenario and situation of the thing or person or action that you desire to be realized, however, from within the detached state. Then in your imagination, while seeing the whole picture, envelop it in the blue light of the Living Sehaji Master, and speak these words with the inner voice, "I turn my desires over to the Holy Spirit for fulfillment." And in this way shall your heart be known, and the Holy Spirit shall begin to work with you to bring what you wish, but in a way that is balanced and karmically neutral and serves the highest spiritual unfoldment of all concerned; for remember, the mark of true Mastery and the highest level of achievement is not the ability to instantly manifest the things of your desires, but to manifest them in an order and progression and manner that is in harmony with all about you and supports of all life and the development and unfoldment of fellow man and the plans of the Holy Spirit and Sugmad. And so, there can sometimes be a delay in the fulfillment of your desires, but this is just the Holy Spirit working on your behalf to have all balance kept and all karma neutrally positioned so your wishes may be had, but not with a price that should cause you necessary return to the physical or lower plane to repay a karmic debt.

The lower planes of this universe of the Sugmad are often called a finished universe. But what does this really mean for the seeker on the path, in terms of his daily life and experiences, and as it does relate to the Law of Assumption as an efficient spiritual law to use? That these planes are already completed means the following:

Over the past thousands of years, as the different inner bodies of man have developed in accordance with their physical manifestation in the human form, the inner planes have been created and formed and enriched with the variety of experience and diversity that does comprise the many varied life forms and creations of this universe.

However, the inner bodies, and the planes where they do reside, do work at a much faster pace as compared with the perception and occurrence of time and events within the lower physical world, for time is elastic, depending on the rate of experience and unfoldment of the person and groups of people in consideration. And so, within the inner worlds, man is not so tied to the density of the physical reality; and so, time does move more quickly there, as lessons and experiences are had and passed through at a much quicker rate, and also the perspective and scope of understanding is much greater, which does also accelerate the pace of unfoldment and experience. But how does this relate to the statement that the lower worlds are a "finished universe?"

As Soul has progressed within the lower inner planes, it has gone far past where the physical consciousness does now reside within its time/experience continuum. However, the inner bodies of man have far surpassed this place and have maximized the development of all those capabilities; and so, the new range of possibility and uncharted realms of exploration within the lower five planes have been exhausted and those planes have been completed in the extent of their sophistication and development. This is why it is now the beginning of the new Age of Man, the Age of Soul or the Heart, for the Age of the Mind has been concluded; and though this faculty still does exist and function, much as do the emotional and causal planes and the bodies they do correspond to, there is no further significant upward development and unfoldment that can occur within this universe of the Sugmad.

That does not mean that man has reached the zenith of his mental capabilities, for this is not the case. It does mean, however, that within this universe, the collective development of all Souls from all galaxies and planets and species has collectively reached the maximum potential and development of all the lower planes. There still does exist capacity for growth of individual Souls on individual planets, as each does unfold and learn and gain experience. But as a universe, the expansion and development of the lower five planes are finished, and this is what is meant by this term.

So what then is the relation to the Law of Assumption? The Law of Assumption works by aligning in coherence all the lower bodies of Soul to quickly and neutrally bring into manifestation the thing that is desired. However, if the lower planes were not well developed and finished, then the frequency patterns and capabilities and rhythms would not be well established and the process would be akin to blazing new trails through the virgin forest. However, since this process and undertaking has been utilized by many who have come before, it is a well established process and law which now can be utilized with ease by those who do now follow. And for this reason, this is a law that works well within this universe, in light of its current state and level of completion of the lower five Planes of God.

The use of Universal Soul Movement to move forward and backward upon the time track and view and see events and potential circumstances is a gift to Soul to better aid it in its journeys and unfoldment. The future of a Soul is a set of probable possibilities according to the life contract of the Soul and what has been agreed to and is necessary. Some events must be experienced, either sooner or later. Some may be avoided. Some have already been experienced and are not to be experienced again. There is an element of choice involved in the timing of the experience, for Soul does always have free will, and some things may be delayed or accelerated according to the desires and wishes of the one who does have to face them, for not all experiences are of a negative nature, and some are very pleasurable and enjoyable to have. And so, Universal Soul Movement is a way to gain perspective and detachment from the events that lie ahead and to have a measure of self-determination and planning, as to what is to be experienced and when, that the Soul's unfoldment and progression might occur at a pace that is comfortable and desirable.

This does not mean, however, that all things are negotiable, for sometimes the Lords of Karma will determine that certain events must occur as planned. But some things may be shifted and repositioned according to the merit and unfoldment of the specific Soul in question. And so, Universal Soul Movement may be well used to travel back along the time track and to see the events and actions that have shaped your current self and situation, and, as well, to travel forward to see what is to come and be able to make informed decisions regarding the challenges and rewards that may be faced in the days and years and lifetimes to come.

The problems and challenges of life are the gifts of Spirit, though in the moment this is surely not always seen to be the case. Human nature being what it is, Soul does not typically strive for unfoldment and growth when all is peaceful and happy and in a state of calm. Soul does respond best when faced with pain and challenges; and so, the problems and issues in life are gifts from Spirit to aid Soul on its way to seek of higher realms, else Soul does rest and remain in place and become stagnant and much time is wasted and the universe does not unfold at the pace and rate that is needed. And so, it is Soul's challenge and test to view the problems it does face as opportunities to learn and grow and aid the plans of Sugmad and keep the universe in balance and headed to the goal.

One of the common errors and frustrations of those who have difficulty manifesting the life they want within the Physical Plane is the tendency and error of focusing on what is feared or sought to be avoided, instead of what is desired. It is a simple case of the law that what you hold in your consciousness and give energy to in the form of emotion and feeling does polarize your energetic field and draws to you that which you do fear most. And so, in this manner are the things you do desire pushed even further away to make room for the objects and situations of your fears to manifest, as is the law and way that must result from the emotional energization of the thought forms which have been created by focusing in the wrong area. And so, the lesson that is so important to learn is to focus the mind and imagination and feelings on the things you do desire and not those that you wish to avoid, and all shall come to you as is the law and the way.

Within your inner bodies your imagination does determine and create all the thought forms and emotions and energetic patterns, which do comprise the energy being that is Soul, you. And so, the reality that is experienced is the cumulative result of the energetic patterns that are created by the imagination at work. And so, the reality each Soul does manifest is an exact result of the imagination and toils of the inner bodies in ways that most are not even conscious or aware of. And the great mistake of man is his belief that he must strive to change his outer acts to change his physical reality, but this is not the case. To change the manifested reality, what first must change are the inner states, and the imagination is the key and main driver of this process and all others. And so, when it is said that the imagination is the key, this is truly so, for it is the driving force and motivator of all that follows after and finally manifests below.

The entire reality of man is created by his own consciousness and the inner bodies of his self. In those of weaker development or less unfoldment or greater unconsciousness of the truth and function of the higher aspect, this can result in confusion and dismay of the results of what is experienced in daily life and living. And truly without the conscious control of the lower bodies they are left to their own devices and may take whatever actions and create whatever karma, they do desire without the steady and enlightened hand of the higher self to guide them in their endeavors. And so, to completely control and become the Master of one's own reality, the full development and unfoldment of the lower bodies and higher aspect is required to have the life that is desired.

To be supreme in your own consciousness is to have reached Self-Realization and be in complete and utter control of all functions and actions of the lower self and the reality it does manifest. This is not to say, however, that all those of the sixth circle and above do now have complete and perfect control and Mastery of their reality. It is a possibility, but not necessarily so, for while each Soul is within its physical shell there always is a variance and fluctuation in the degree and proficiency with which the initiations are used. And so, though one may have achieved the fifth or sixth circle, there still may be times when that Soul is asleep or not fully using to the maximum of its capabilities the powers it does have. However, with time and practice this proficiency is gained and by degree it does become more skilled in creating and maintaining the reality it does seek, until finally the control and development of the inner bodies is so complete that all that does occur within its reality is known and understood and seen, and this is the goal of all life within the lower planes of the Sugmad.

"Inner talking" can be said and described as the practice of conversing and instructing the inner bodies of man to constantly train and bring them into a state of coherence with the goals and wishes of Soul. It is the practice of affirming and describing what is the goal and method of operation, which each body should clearly see and understand what is expected of it to succeed in its mission and responsibilities. This does finally lead, as it is successful, to greater levels of knowingness and beingness, as the inner bodies do become aligned and coherent and the truth of Soul is able to penetrate and share the love and light of the pure worlds above the Great Divide.

To practice this means of unfoldment and the making of good progress, one must enter into quiet contemplation by using the secret word. Then call to the inner bodies and assemble them in front of you, and begin the dialogue and discussion to hear the thoughts and trials of each, and to instruct each in its duties and responsibilities and course of proper action. And in this way will the inner bodies learn and grow, and this inner dialogue will be a powerful tool to aid you in your endeavors and struggles upon the path.

Each Soul experiences the reality that is manifested out of its own energetic bodies and patterns and vibrations. However, if the inner bodies are not disciplined and creating actively the physical reality that is desired, then a reality may be assigned and dictated to it by the one who is responsible for its guidance and protection. Each Soul is assigned and part of some Hierarchy or Order within the inner planes. And it is the responsibility of that Hierarchy or Order to ensure that the Soul is playing the role and fulfilling the obligations of which it is required. And so, if the Soul is not actively creating the reality of its own desires and wishes, then a reality is assigned to it until it is at a place where it can assume responsibility for its own affairs and deeds.

Indeed, one of the benefits of being a student of The Way of Truth is that the Holy Spirit and the Living Sehaji Master do together work on the student's behalf to create a flow of reality that will speed the progress of the student in his unfoldment and development, in the most rapid and efficient manner possible, without overwhelming its resources or abilities to speed each Soul on its path back home, and return it to that state of Self-Realization where it is able to finally assume complete responsibility for the reality it does experience. And so, this is why it is important to strive and work to develop and master the lower bodies, for this is the key to freedom and the ability to manifest the reality of your desires and wishes, and not one that is assigned to you without your knowledge or conscious consent. However, all of this must follow in accordance and agreement with the will and plans of the Sugmad's heart above.

Enlightenment, or Self-Realization, is a personal thing to be judged by one's own self, and never subject to the musings or evaluation of any other, for the opinions and judgments of others bring you no aid, nor bear any merit, within the heavens above. Your development and achievement of spiritual goals and milestones is between you and the Sugmad and no other. And for this reason, it is most important that you evaluate your success only within your heart and the truth that you do know as your own, and not by any other.

For if you rely on the confirmation of others to judge of your achievement, then, you remain bound by the dictates of the lower world, and never are you truly master of your own reality and accord. And so, it must always be remembered that you are to judge the progress made and achievements gained only by your own heart, and never by any other. For the truth, as you do live and experience it, is what guides the reality of your life and living, and in the end, this is the only thing that matters.

The Law of Silence is truly difficult for many enthusiastic seekers on the path, for it is a natural thing to wish to share the experiences and truth that have been revealed to one who seeks of God. Yet this is a law that is well to be observed, if the seeker does wish to make certain rapid progress on the path. The Law of Silence is this: When the seeker is directly spoken to or instructed by the Living Sehaji Master, or any other Master of the Order of the Sehaji, what is said to him is for his ears and no other, for the truth or guidance that is given is spoken and worded and energetically charged in such a way as to be specific to that individual, only. And when this truth is received and held within the heart, it does have the effect of raising the vibration of the inner bodies and facilitating the purifying process of Soul within the lower realms. But what then can be shared, and under what circumstances?

The safest rule to follow is to ask the Master if there is any doubt as to whether or not the experience and information may be shared. The next general rules of thumb are these: Within the discussion classes which are opened with the HU and the invocation of the Master's presence, there is created a sacred space in which the energy is focused and contained, and what is shared and kept within that space is protected and may be spoken. However, all students must understand that the Law of Silence does apply outside the discussion class, and the words and experiences recounted should not be repeated again. The other situation in which it is safe to share is with an initiate of the fifth circle or above, for those of this merit and achievement do have the skill and ability to hold and return the energy that does come with the sharing of the gift. And so, by the application of this law shall the student make great progress on the path and return more swiftly to the heart of the Sugmad.

Spiritual knowledge and love are disseminated in ways that are of two methods and means. First, as general truths and principles that may be shared with all concerned, and that do embody the truths, they may be understood by a range of consciousnesses and abilities. The Law of Silence does not apply in this case, for the energetic coding and vortices attached are such that they may be sustained no matter to whom they are revealed. The second type of spiritual knowledge and love is keyed specifically to the one receiving it, and it is to the student to learn the subtle art and skill of discernment to know which is which and to what words and experiences the Law of Silence does apply.

"Illumination" is an ancient term to describe those Souls who have achieved that level of accomplishment in the spiritual hierarchies where they do begin to radiate a love that can be felt and sometimes seen by others. It is a state that is not specific to any level of initiation, but does refer to the ability to project the love and light of God through the lower bodies to be felt and experienced by those in the Physical Plane. Typically the term has referred to the "Illumined saints or Masters." However, this is an ambiguous term, for what was considered a saint or Master in terms of spiritual accomplishment and initiation within the physical realm has changed and evolved over the many centuries and millennia, and one who walks and bears the light of a seventh or eighth initiate, today, might have only been a second initiate 2,000 years ago. And so, this is a term whose technical meaning and substance and definition have changed greatly over the years.

However, in general, it can be defined as one who possesses sufficient merit, wisdom and accomplishment to be a clear channel for the love and power and light of God, that his or her presence and proximity does burn away the dross and darkness of illusion from the clouded eyes of those who are near to him, in such a manner that greater truth and light is recognized and experienced. This can vary greatly in degree and effect, but to be "illumined" is to know and see and have experienced and be consciously able to wield the light and power and wisdom of God, and this could be done by any above the second circle, if they did have the experience and merit and ability.

And so, the greater challenge is not to merely experience, and for a brief moment become, one of the illumined states, but to constantly dwell in it and embody it as the whole and entire essence of your being in all that you do and say. And generally, today, to be able to walk and live in this state does require a level of initiation exceeding the eighth plane or above, though any above the second could occasionally ascend to and experience this state of being. And so, for the one who has reached permanently this exalted state, life is free of illusions and clear before the eyes, and no darkness or negativity can cloud the vision or judgment in any challenge or difficulty or situation that is faced. And so, life does become a transparent and enjoyable adventure and journey through the obstacles and illusions and joys that do comprise the experiences within the physical realm.

The sum total of purpose and intent of this section of the truth and light of God's word is to aid the student to develop within himself the tools and capabilities to unlock the secret keys to wisdom, power and love that are locked within the heart and waiting to be released. And always, it must be remembered that love is the only goal and the most important thing, for, without it, all secret esoteric knowledge and lore are as inconsequential as a power drill without any electricity. Love is the power that drives all life; and so, as the techniques, and truths are wielded, to gain of greater heights and spiritual achievement, always remember this. Love is the heart of the matter and the most important thing. And if you do always keep this as your goal and objective, you never shall fail in anything you do endeavor.

Chapter Six

The Love of the HU

HU is the sacred gift from the Sugmad to the great Souls of this universe that are ready to receive of the heart of Its truth. It is the final key to the highest plane in the long journey through all the lower realms of this universe and back to the heart of God in the Ocean of Love and Mercy. For those who deeply love Spirit and truth, then HU becomes the beacon by which their way is lit and guided and all other actions taken to follow where it leads. To truly love HU means to open all aspects of one's life and love and presence in every word that is spoken and every action that is taken in this plane and world or any other. HU is the key to man's return, and for those who truly love it and make it a part of themselves, they shall find ultimate success in their endeavors and trials along the path.

The Sugmad chose the HU for one very simple reason. It is the cumulative and net sound of all other sounds, vibrations and frequencies combined in one and refined to its pure essence as a Master key to unlock the doors to each and every plane. Just as a locksmith creates specific keys for specific rooms, there are secret words and mantras to open specific planes and secret places in the universe. But like the Master locksmith as well, he does create one key that is so subtle and perfect in design it will open any door to any room in which it is inserted. And so, the HU is such a key and may be used to take the wielder to any place within the universe that he does have the merit and the ability to go.

Though the student may ask the question of why other words are needed in addition to the HU, there are very good reasons why this must be the case. The HU, though it can open every door as needed, does guide the student in a general way and can make specific journeys difficult or more complicated than need be. The secret words of the initiations do serve to identify your specific rank as Soul when you do travel to inner realms. And though the HU could be used to take you to the temple you do seek, without the proper identification of your merit and your rank, you yet may be refused the entrance you desire. As well, the secret words relate to specific energetic pathways and gates that are well known and traveled by others before. And this can make the success and ease of the intention much greater than otherwise it might be, if only the general power of the HU were used to go and seek the destination of your heart. And so, as the student progresses on the path, one of the things he learns is when it is best to use the word of HU on general occasions or to manifest the Holy Spirit for protection from dark places, and when a specific word is used to follow a line of energy and safely and rapidly arrive at your goal and destination.

Also was this sacred word selected and chosen for its properties of aggregating light and transforming darkness, for like the alchemist's stone, it is the key to turning spiritual lead to gold and transmuting the dross of negativity and illusion into the heart of love and light. The HU is the water, the universal solvent of all negativity and pain and suffering. And so, for whatever trial is faced, whatever challenge rendered unto Soul, the HU is given by Sugmad to light the way and open the heart to the path of higher understanding and love and the ability to take of proper action to guide the Soul back home.

When the HU is sung, the Master frequency encoded in its many layers is transferred and becomes a part of the energetic bodies of man; and so, just as the HU is the universal key to all life and the common denominator of existence in this universe, so does the student become connected to all life when this sacred word is sung and he becomes part of it and is, for a brief moment in time, connected to and enmeshed in the very fabric of existence and the heart of all life and all things. And so, the HU is the key to connecting to the heart of the universe, and this always should be remembered when it is sung and the vistas of heaven are opened to the student.

Sri Rama (spoken directly and verbatim)

When I was still a student within the physical shell and only just embarking on my studies of the great works and truths of The Way of Truth, my Master did take me to a mountaintop and there he made me sit and told me to be still and listen. As I sat and intently peered my ear into the sky, I began to hear of all the sounds of life and living about me: the birds, the wind, the water, the leaves... and I began to listen so hard I even did hear my own heartbeat as it pounded within my chest. And so, focused was I on listening that I did barely notice the failure of my eyes to see the plains spread out before me, and instead I began to notice the sparkling stars above as they hung within a moonless sky.

And all at once I was engulfed with the rushing winds and powerful movement of the universe swimming about me as I was tossed about on its currents and eddies, and I was aware of, and consumed by, the sound that was all others. And as the rushing did subside, I did hear the gentle HU, like the melody of a harp that was played to sing the song of God's heart. And as the ecstasy and bliss of my pure beingness overwhelmed me, I instantly did awake and found myself again on the mountaintop, my Master there beside me with a smile on his face. And he did say to me: "This is the sound of HU. It is the heart of God's voice and the key to all the heavens and the wisdom you do seek. Remember it always and keep it near your heart, and it shall always protect you and keep you safe from harm." And then we rose and returned to the village below, but my heart and reality were forever changed, for I now had experienced the love of God and found the key to my way back to his home.

I did continue in my training for a period of another 12 years after my experience on the mountain, and in that time I did learn of many secrets and the truths of the path back home to God. And after I did finally receive of my initiation into the circle of our Brotherhood, I did accept my mission and set out upon the lands to spread the teachings of The Way of Truth, though this is not the name by which they were known in this ancient time and place. And so, over the course of many years and travels, I did cross of many plains and seas and mountains, to Germany, Persia and even to India to spread the teachings of the Light and Sound to those few who were ready to hear its truth and study of its ways.

When I did finally release my shell to move on to other regions, Milarepa himself did come to aid me with the transfer to the other side. And after a brief repose he did guide me to the mountains, and to the monastery of Agam Des for further training and instruction in the secret arts and mysteries that I would need to know to continue in my efforts of service within the inner realms.

At Agam Des I did have the good fortune to be taught and introduced to many of the greatest Masters of our time, for this was a great honor for me to be received into their company and into their hearts, and I was greatly overjoyed at the opportunity I was given to study at their knee. Among those of their number who came to tutor me were Milati, Quetzacoatl, Tindor Saki, Gopal Das, the great Kal, Marpa and many others too numerous to list who were kind and gracious enough to teach me of the hidden ways and secrets of the lessons they had learned.

I did study at Agam Des for quite some time after my translation, but then after the passage of perhaps 200 years or so, it was time to again return and continue with my mission. And so, I did descend to Earth to serve there once again. However, this time my training was less lengthy, as I had been well prepared in advance, and with my previous experience as a Living Sehaji Master on the Earth. And so, a period of only three or four years was truly required before I did assume the mantle and did receive the Rod of Power, for the abilities of a Soul on Earth have little to do with its experience in that specific lifetime and everything to do with the training it has received in the time that came before from within the inner worlds or other many lifetimes past.

And so, in my second incarnation in the role of the Living Sehaji Master, it was not a difficult thing to quickly progress and unfold and receive the Rod of Power, although this was not a common occurrence at this time and many did have difficulty believing that it was truly so. But their hearts and the power of my words and truth and abilities soon convinced them of what was so and I was able to proceed onward with my mission.

The Rod of Power at this time was given by Milarepa as the head of the Grand Council of the Sehaji. I was taken out of the body as I slept one night and awoke in the Valley of Tirmer, as it is the location and tradition for the passing to occur. I do not recall the exact date, and it is not important, for when the Holy Spirit does hear of the Sugmad's heart and knows it is the time for change, then the Silent Nine do go to Milarepa and summon all the Brothers to the valley for the event.

And under the moonlit sky, in the quiet of the valley, with all our Order gathered round, the Rod was manifested by Milarepa from the hand of the Silent Nine who did bear it to his heart, and as the sacred words were spoken, I knelt before his knee and raised my arms to him, and with a clap of thunder, which nearly all the heavens split, the final word was uttered and he did hand to me the Rod of Power of the Holy Spirit and I did receive the mantle and my mission was begun.

When I did return to my body and in my physical consciousness awake, it did seem a morning like any other, except for one certain thing: that I now could feel the pressure of the power as it did weigh down on me. And over the course of the successive weeks and months I learned of my new abilities and strengths and the many things of which I was capable; and so, my mission had begun, with little external fanfare or trumpets, and I quietly began to work to spread the love and truth of the Holy Spirit.

The transfer of the Rod of Power from Wah Z to Dan Rin was an entirely different matter. When I did receive the Rod, though some of our Order did feel that I needed more physical years in my shell before I was ready to wield the power, none did dissent or disagree with the choice that had been made, because the Master who had come before me was ready and willing and desirous to relinquish the Rod, as he was concluded in his mission and desired to commence to other realms, and so, the transfer was completed with little controversy or incident.

Wah Z, on the other hand, did wish to select his own successor, and this is where our paths do diverge, for many of the Council did believe that Wah Z should have the right to designate his own successor, as he did desire to do, and others, however, and Milarepa and the Nine among them, did disagree and felt it was a choice left to Sugmad to designate and confer the mantle as It did see fit and desire. And so, the Council was divided between Wah Z and Dan Rin. However, in the final moment the Nine and Sugmad did prevail, but it was not a gentle night.

As Dan Rin knelt to receive the Rod from Milarepa, a great shout went out from the Brotherhood assembled and a stream of the Sehaji descended upon the valley to dispute the claim of right to the One selected to receive the Rod. And a great battle did ensue, for the Sehaji Masters in dispute had all brought with them their legions to defend what they did see as the right and proper action which Wah Z sought to take, to control the future and destiny of the former path of the Light and Sound. And so, the Red Dragon Guard, the defenders of the Light and Sound of the HU did descend as they were summoned by the Nine and Milarepa, and the battle did rage and ensue with such intensity and duration that all the heavens shook and it did seem that the very sky would split and all would come to ruin. But finally the Red Dragons did begin to resume order and control, and without haste Milarepa did conclude the ceremony and Dan Rin was given the Rod and named as the Living Sehaji Master.

However, the debate over the decision of Milarepa and the Nine did continue for some time, at the instigation and prodding of Wah Z and those who served with him on Earth. However, this was only the challenge of their training and a test for them as well, to continue on their path and in their way. And eventually the higher aspect of Wah Z and the other Sehaji Masters did see the wisdom of the course that was taken and finally did concede that Dan Rin was the proper choice, and so, moved to consolidate and support his mission and turn. But the echoes of this turmoil and division did eventually reach the Physical Plane, and it was some time, and after similar battles and confusion, that Dan Rin was recognized on Earth and his mission was begun.

So, the important thing to remember is that no matter how high a Soul does climb upon the ladder to God while in the physical body and even beyond, there are always the tests of love and wisdom that ever must be passed to ascend to greater heights and continue on the path. And though the lessons may vary in difficulty and magnitude, to the Souls that experience them, they are tests nonetheless and none are immune or ever able to escape the lessons that are the gift of Spirit to aid the student on the path, even when he has become a Master.

Sri Rumi (spoken directly and verbatim)

The Way of Truth was first put to written form during my time and mission upon the Earth, though it was not called by that name which Paulji selected for it, as was given by the Sugmad. For during my time the consciousness and people and culture and language and academic and religious customs of the day did differ greatly from today. And so, after my years of instruction from Shamus i Tabriz, whom I met along the road, I did set about to fully and truthfully record the wisdom and love and experience of God that I had been given and received.

And so, as there was not the vocabulary or proper semantic structure for me to write in technical, esoteric terms, for neither would those sentences have been understood by man of that time, and since it was my mission to write for all to read and listen and know and benefit and not just the priests or university students, I did choose and was instructed to write the wisdom I did know and teach it in verse and rhyme and poetry, as this was the way and custom that the common man and family would remember and understand.

And so, as I did have the mantle and the permanent connection to the Holy Spirit, I let the love and truth flow through me and find the words and forms that It sought to reach the hearts of man, for I did listen and repeat and was the vehicle for expression, but I was not the one who created the thoughts or initiated the thinking, for the truth that came from my heart and lips came from a much higher place, far above the Mental Plane.

99

And so, the training of Shamus i Tabriz was for me, to be the first avatar of my kind, and to bring the words of love and truth and power down into the physical realm, that all should hear and read their words, and know that God exists, and that It does love Its many sons and daughters down below and ever would be there watching over to aid them in their journey and welcome them back home.

The Masters that influenced and guided me to aid me in my mission to, for the first time, commit the wisdom of the Holy Spirit to written form, were first, of course, Shamus i Tabriz, about whom much is known and written, but as well the other Masters from within our Order and our Brotherhood who serve the great White line, including Gopal Das, Mithra, Pythagoras, Vishnu and others who do remain hidden and who I cannot name, for the time is not yet right for their names and identities to be known and uttered, for I did come from a universe far away and with many old friends. I had long wandered the many universes of the Great God and Father of the Sugmad, collecting of the wisdom and truth, as it was known, and bringing all I did see and remember to Earth back in that time, for I was a son of the love of creation, and one who was known and loved by many beyond the seas; and so, it was my great love of man and my wish to see him risen that I did come and take a body, and give the gift I gave.

When the works of The Way of Truth were finally placed in written form, it grounded the powerful God-energy within the Physical Plane in a way that never had been done before, for the Physical Plane was now ready and could withstand the power of this love, whereas, before, when it was only an oral tradition, the power had been brought down but had quickly dissipated and spread as the words and memories faded. But man was now ready for the next step in his evolution; and so, I truly came and brought the words to writing, that the energy and power would remain and activate the vortices and consciousness of the Earth, that that great age might be initiated and the unfoldment and development might again continue to succeed with best-laid plans.

And so, though the inner structure of The Way of Truth within the heavens above did remain essentially unchanged, within the

Physical Plane the seeds were now planted and begun for the birth of great traditions to aid the rise of man. And so, many would come after and teach the works of The Way of Truth in the form and language and with the name and title that was relevant and proper for the times and culture they served. And thus was the pure God-power released upon the Earth and given a permanent connection through the words that I did write.

Leytor (spoken directly and verbatim)

To be one with the HU is an esoteric sounding concept but an important skill to realize if one is ever to truly ascend to the top of the mountain. The HU is life, the universe, the key and passport to all travel and power and love. And so, to become one with it means to remove all impurities and dross such that the purity and essence of the nature of the HU, of creation, of ultimate power and love is reflected and mirrored by the energetic signature of the student.

Now, of course, this is not an easy task, for it is the goal of illumination and Mastership, and if it were easily achieved then there should be no purpose or meaning to the trials down below. However, it truly can be achieved and should be always strived for, for this state does represent the most desired one of perfection, perfect freedom, perfect love, and perfect power. And so, the student, when practicing the spiritual exercises and singing the sacred HU, aloud or to oneself, does connect to its vibration and remove of more dross and impurity with each step and effort and thus is closer brought to the state of perfect harmony and resemblance that is the final goal within this universe of the Sugmad.

The Sugmad can feel and know the waves and currents of the collective consciousnesses of all within its reaches; however, it is mainly concerned with balance and progression on a larger scale, and so does not involve Itself in the struggle of the physical embodiments of man and other creatures, except in extreme instances of imbalance or when It does involve a Soul of greatest merit such as the Living Sehaji Master or some other Master, for it is not within the Sugmad's abilities to incarnate within the Physical

Plane, for it is not a thing that would be possible to do without destroying all that exists within that range of coarse vibrations.

And, too, the ignorance and error of the backward ways of man does not make it a suitable candidate for the presence and instruction of the Sugmad, for there are other matters of greater concern that must be dealt with and addressed. And so, it is left to the great love that is born by the Living Sehaji Master and the Masters and other saviors and great Souls who love all life and man, that they will descend to human shells and serve the ones they love in the physical world below.

The spiritual and the physical represent the spectrum of polarity within the Physical Plane between the positive and the negative forces, the truth and Maya or illusion; and so, the way to the heart of God from within the lower planes is the way of perfect balance and truth, and this is where the love and teachings of The Way of Truth are found to guide the seeker home.

Maya, or illusion, exists within the lower realms, and to deny or ignore this fact is to live in imbalance and within only the positive force. And in terms of progress home, this is just as detrimental a hindrance as to live wholly within the negative, for it is just an equal expression of ignorance, however, of an opposite polarity. And so, the goals of The Way of Truth and the teachings and example of the Masters are to teach the student balance and to find the middle path and follow it back home to the heart of the Sugmad.

This is the great struggle that leads to the Great Divide and confrontation between the children of The Way of Truth, of wisdom, balance and truth, against the children of Kal, or the extremes of polarization to the dark and to the light, for the Kal does not only embody the negative aspect, but the positive as well, when it is expressed in an out-of-balance fashion. And though this is a point that is little understood, it is an important one to note. The Kal is not only of the negative nature but the positive as well, and its presence and manifestation is in the unbalanced expression of either, to lead the seeker astray and further from the path.

All Souls are children of The Way of Truth in the final analysis and classification; however, as Souls do travel and walk upon the path throughout the lower realms, some must at times serve of the will and desires of the Kal, that illusion should be wielded and balance should be kept and each Soul might receive the lesson and karma that he does need to aid him on the path. And so, within the dual worlds the battle always rages between those Souls who do the will of the Holy Spirit and those who do the will of the Kal. And these are not permanent roles or designations, only the temporary names they are given to describe their immediate position as they do learn and grow and progress along the path.

And so, those who do proclaim to be healers, saints, saviors, psychics or others who serve the Light of God must be viewed with detached skepticism and careful ponderance, for wielding of the light in an out-of-balance fashion is to be mired in, and sharing of, the Kal in an equal fashion, and in service of illusion, for the goal should always be to walk the middle path in perfect balance and harmony, and following the truth and light of God, and in this way shall no karma be created and all shall be achieved and the Soul shall soon find its way back to heaven.

The Vi Guru is the Living Sehaji Master, and to have his clear vision is to be able to clearly see behind any mask of illusion that does exist within the worlds of God and to be able to know and understand the purpose and the meaning before all that passes before his eyes, for illusion and action begets yet greater illusion, and this is how the lower planes are developed and maintained; and so, the vision of the Master does have the opposite effect, for the clear vision of the Vi Guru does see what must be done to take of proper action, that illusion might be dissolved and the light and truth of God may shine through. And so, it is the power and ability of those with this clear vision to see beneath the surface and in any situation take the action that is right to eliminate all illusion and bring into this plane the pure light and truth of God to aid of all of man.

The trials of the cave of fire and water are the journey the student must take before receiving the second initiation and the permanent connection to the Holy Spirit. During these trials, the student does

103

alternate between the fires of challenge and difficulty and the soothing waters of understanding and wisdom gained. And so, this period of time is known by this name for the intensity and duration and frequency of the many challenges that must be faced and overcome before the student may be given the second initiation.

Within the inner realms as well, this is also a real location and pathway to the realms of the second plane, and in the finer bodies the student must find his way and have the courage to face the fiery illusions of his fears to reach the soothing waters of the lake that separates the two planes, for the second circle may not be gained if the student still has any fear or attachment to the illusions of the lower Physical Planes, nor of the soothing water and love of Sugmad in the form of the great lake. And so, at night in dreams or in quiet contemplation the student is taken through these trials, and it may be consciously remembered and experienced or may not, depending on the student and the lessons that need to be learned. But before the permanent connection to the Holy Spirit may be given, this is the test and trial that must be passed to continue on the journey home.

The concept and direction of self-surrender to Spirit does not in any way imply passivity or complacency. Spirit seeks those who love their fellow man and are willing to work on Its behalf to serve their teaching and progression. And so, self-surrender means that the one is able and willing to hear the instructions and subtle prodding, as Spirit does guide it in Its actions to serve Its will and plans. But then it is the responsibility and duty and mission of the student to go and do what has been said and instructed and not to passively lie about and declare this self-surrender. Spirit and love and power and truth exist within the lower realms to aid man in his journey, and self-surrender means to become an active participant in hearing of Its will and wishes and doing what must be done to aid of all of man.

The Godman on Earth has the responsibility and duty to uphold, embrace and embody the perfect adherence of Divine Law. The actions of the Godman set the example, both in the inner worlds and in the physical, as to what is expected and appropriate in the ways of action and duty to the Divine Laws of God. And if the

Godman is not perfect in his adherence to these laws of the Sugmad, then an opening and crack is created for the darkness to attach and find footing, and error and improper action does begin to propagate and grow within the many planes and worlds of this universe.

And when the Godman is acting in perfect harmony and in accordance with Divine Law, then this sets the precedent and example and energetic template of what should be done and how the actions of life must be taken to move farther toward the goal. And so, it is the challenge and test of the Godman to in every action and deed know and adhere to Divine Law in its highest level and truth, for otherwise the universe is set in imbalance and the great trials and pains of illusion must further continue on.

The middle eye is the gateway for the vision of truth and the inner worlds of God, and it is keyed and locked to prevent the opening and vision of those who are not yet ready to see; and so, when the HU is sung and the spiritual exercises practiced, the subtle bodies are refined and removed of dross and impurities, and man is brought to a greater level of understanding and closer to the goal. And once a sufficient level of maturity and awareness is reached, then, the spiritual eye shall open in a timely and normal way, to further aid the student along his path and return home. But the singing of the HU and the spiritual exercises are the fastest way to clear the bodies and quickly move to that place that the student is ready to have his eye opened and see the mysterious glories of God.

Love and detached goodwill are the balanced state of existence sought to open the heart of God and find oneself again at Its door and in Its arms; and so, the HU is the key and template to finding and understanding this state within the heart of the student. When the HU is sung with love, then the heart begins to flower and open like the petals of a rose, and as this center opens and the resonance is established, then the Holy Spirit is moved to become a pattern and imprint for the frequency of the heart which is in alignment with the essence of the Sugmad.

And it is this mirror vibration and pattern that is the key to greater love and understanding and power and wisdom that are the fruits that are sought in the journey back above; and so, the student should always seek to find and place the HU within his heart, for in this manner shall the perfect balance of detached goodwill and love be achieved and the student shall be sped back upon the path to God.

When a body dies and the Soul is transferred back to the higher consciousness, then the physical consciousness is expelled and only the higher state experienced. This is the same thing which occurs when the HU is sung and the contemplative exercises are done daily, except that the physical shell remains alive and living, for when the HU is sung and contemplation undertaken with success, then the Soul is lifted far above the human consciousness and into the heart and love of the Sugmad, even if he is not aware of this occurrence. And so, it can be truly said that the diligent and committed Way of Truth student does "die daily," for in his journeys and his travels it is the similar thing to what occurs when the physical shell and time on Earth are finally depleted and the Soul does go and move on.

The Godman is the living, walking incarnation and presence of the face of God on Earth, of It and of Its essence and truth, but not It, Itself. The Godman is the embodiment of the living presence of Sugmad within a physical shell to the utmost degree and capability that is possible within this universe. And so, to look upon the Godman is to gaze upon the face of a living God within the Physical Plane. And the love seen and felt in darshan, and the wisdom and truth given by his heart, are a gift and a temptation to show the student what may be expected when he does return to the heavens above. And so, when one does gaze upon the face and eyes of the Godman, the heart should be opened with joy, for the face of a living God has truly been seen, and this is a blessing and gift for all who are able to have this opportunity.

Souls who have reached a level of achievement where they are connected to and do receive the love of the Sugmad have paid sufficient of their karmic debts, and cleared the lower bodies, that they have earned the right to have the love of Sugmad forever felt in their hearts. However, the majority of all Souls do incur such great karma accumulated over many lifetimes of ignorance and error that it never could be repaid and undone. And so, the grace of the Sugmad, as given through the Master, can lessen the karmic burden and increase the worthiness of Soul to receive Its love and connection, for the Masters are able and skilled at evaluating the student and their Soul records and past inclinations and deciding to give of grace to aid them on their way. And for the student this does mean that a Soul, who might be bound by four or five lifetimes of heavy karma, may see it resolved in one because the Master will, through his grace, as given by the Sugmad, take a piece of the karma and burn it off himself by passing it into the great life current of the Holy Spirit for dissolution in some far corner of the universe where it can cause no other Soul harm. And so, the question of the worthiness of a Soul to receive the love of Sugmad can be lessened and ameliorated by the grace of Its own heart as given by the Master to those who are committed to the path and honest and genuine in their efforts to succeed in their endeavors and serve the will of the Sugmad.

The traditional customs of seeking to connect with the Sugmad through the various traditions and paths, including fasting, prayer, recitation, complex yogic sutras, isolation or other forms of penance and supplication are all transcended by the singing of the HU. All other forms and methods are like using a 20-watt light bulb to find your way to the moon, while the HU contains such power and perfection that it is a laser beam of cobalt blue to guide you truly through the night. The power and purification are such that, although the other ways may yield success over time and in some small measure, the HU is the surest way to rapidly climb the mountain and return to the heart of God in this lifetime alone.

The nature of the HU is such that it is the universal base frequency and building block for all other holy words, mantras, prayers and other forms of audible expression used to seek the heart of God. The HU represents the purest element of God, truth and existence, and it is for this reason that it does have such power and the ability to do what it can do to cleanse the lower bodies and free the Soul from darkness and the illusion that binds it here. And so, it can be best said and described that the HU is the linguistic frequency of the Light and Sound Itself, and the basis and true heart upon which all others of merit and valor and truth are built. And so, this is the gift now given to the children upon the Earth, for now the time is come to take the next step forward, and the HU is the basic foundation and building block to start all Souls on their way in this last leg of the journey.

Chapter Seven

The Way to Know the Heart

Leytor (spoken directly and verbatim)

Peace of heart is a state of joy and ecstasy often told of and referred to, but rarely known and felt by those not committed to the path. It is that state which is known and exists when the heart is opened to the love and light and power of the higher self and worlds, and this pure power and truth of God does flow through the heart and into the lower bodies and the physical world that surrounds it. The peace of heart means that the state of perfect neutrality and love and detachment has been achieved, that there is no blockage of the flow of energy from within the higher realms, and this great calm brings a joy and ecstasy such as cannot otherwise be known and felt within the lower realms. And so, the student on the path should, for this reason, always seek to be gentle and open his heart, for through the spiritual exercises of The Way of Truth, the perfect state of calm and detachment may be received, and the glory and wisdom and power of God felt and had within this realm.

The ego, or the dominant expression of the self, which comprises the composite of the lower bodies below the Great Divide, has as its mission and purpose to keep man mired in the illusion of the lower worlds and safe from the liberating truth of God's love. And so, the ego does, in all its machinations of self-importance and delusion, cause the body of man to think that the love of God cannot be obtained and won. But this is not the case, for the heart does know and recognize the higher truth when it is seen and felt. And so, in the course of daily affairs and struggles, it is the constant test of man within the lower realms to keep of certain detachment and balance, that the truth of wisdom and light may be seen and recognized and known by the heart. For when the ego or mind does begin to assert itself as the highest level of existence and achievement, then, this is the sign that the negative forces are at play and laboring to keep the truth from your heart and higher purpose.

For daily practice to rid the self of ego and Maya and illusion, the following techniques may be practiced. First, each day at rising, or when beginning preparations for work, or to begin each daily undertaking, take a quiet moment alone and gently sing the HU or the sacred word of your initiation to polarize your subtle bodies with the radiance and love of God. And then, after a few moments, declare within yourself that you seek to see and experience only truth within this day. And with practice and diligence the lower bodies shall begin to be trained to repel the negative forces and keep The Way of Truth well lit.

A second technique that may be used to see the truth within illusion and keep the heart free from distractions is, when you do encounter some difficulty or obstacle upon your path of daily living, to quietly to yourself sing five of the sacred HUs and then in your imagination, ask the Master to come to you and sweep away any illusion and show you only truth, that your heart should not become obstructed, and you might only know the peace and joy and ecstasy that comes from an open heart and a connection to Sugmad's love. These are two simple ways of daily practice to keep the heart open and clear to hear and feel the love and truth of Sugmad.

The heart does bear burdens and concerns which are given to it by the mind to cloud the flow of truth and wisdom from above and to keep it swept below the rug of illusion that the ego seeks to lay to bury all hope of escape from the mortal shell and Wheel of 84. And so, the way to free the heart is to dissolve the seeds of illusion and Maya that the mind does truly plant there. And this is done through the diligent and repeated practice of the spiritual exercises of The Way of Truth. For when the spiritual exercises are practiced, the heart is opened and does connect to the purifying love and power of the light of higher realms. And since the seeds

110

of mind are comprised of the stuff of illusion, no darkness may remain where an open heart exists; and so, the illusions must be expelled and the heart cleared and opened until the mind does try again. And so, it is a process of determination to continue in the works and spiritual exercises until the mind is trained and the heart is released and shall remain forever open to the wisdom from above.

Life, real life, is lived and experienced above the Great Divide in the worlds of beingness. And although we are here in this life in this plane, and this is a reality of life, as well, the real understanding and forces of occurrence and cause do come from far above. And so, the most the mind can ever do is evaluate and analyze of existing circumstances and results, but never the root cause, for this does come from a source and place that only the heart can go. And so, for the seeker who desires to have of perfect understanding and wisdom, the mental body is not the answer to his prayers, for that is like using one effect to analyze another, and never can this work or succeed.

Instead, to truly understand, the root cause and first movement must be sought and known, and it is only the heart that can succeed in this endeavor. And so, to those who resort to the powers of the Mental Plane to achieve of their objectives, there is this to say; that body and plane do not have the capacity to understand the infinite complexity that supersedes it. And so, in the end, the seeker must come to know and understand that only through the heart can the greater truth be known, for this is the only way the lower bodies may access and truly gain the wisdom of the heavens.

Within the different ages of man there are waves of frequencies and light that are brought and integrated into the lower selves as he does grow and unfold. And always is this wisdom given through the heart, though it may be used to activate and develop others of the lower bodies, if it is their time and place. And so, now, as the Age of the Mind does end and diminish, the highest plane of this universe is now developed and mature; and so, the next great age is ready to begin before the ages close and the Kali Yuga does come to an end. For it is no coincidence that the darkest age of man is also the one in which he faces his greatest test, to gain of his heart and hear the golden wisdom that is given to him from above.

And so, as the Age of the Heart opens and is begun again with the arrival of the new Master, the consciousnesses of man on Earth have been prepared for this final test and challenge, and as the truth and wisdom from various paths is given and received, the hearts of those who are ready and prepared to journey on shall recognize the love and truth that is born upon those pages and hear of what is said. For the heart is like a direct delivery mechanism for Sugmad to send to Its beloved sons and daughters the truth of Its own heart. And so, all who are currently incarnated here on Earth or waiting up above do have the opportunity and ability to hear what is given and said and pass the tests and continue on. For the wisdom, compassion, love and mercy of those who walk on Earth is a direct result of the waves of frequency and unfoldment sent to all Souls below by the One who watches over all from the Ocean of Love and Mercy above. And so, this is why you do see the beginnings of a change and shift in perception as greater truth and light is sent below. And as the new age commences and furthers in its days, the truth and love of the Sugmad shall be given for all to seek and hold and bring into their hearts to find their true way home.

One of the greatest keys to Self-Realization and God-Realization is the humility of the student, for this is a rapid way to clear the mind and open of the heart. When the mind does try to assert itself, and speak of its prominence and importance, then this is the key and signal to gently put to rest its ambitions and boasts, and to allow yourself to find the peace and quiet of humility that shall return you to the path and the detachment and balanced neutrality that is necessary to ascend the ladder of God. And so, to cultivate the vitality of this virtue within the heart the seeker should always remember and never forget that when the ego does assert itself as the master of its domain, then gently to release it and allow it to go on its way, for this is not the path of one who is truly on his way.

The heart is the only instrument of man capable of realizing the truth of God and the universes below. And in my long journey to Mastership, the many lessons I did fail were the ones when I did listen to my mind and not my heart, for the greatest wisdom of man is that which is given from above, and which only may be found in the subtle murmurings and true ways of the heart. And so, I would spend many nights in quiet contemplation, seeking to quiet my fears and the racing of my mind until at last I did begin to achieve of the success which I had sought. And gradually and by degree, the chattering of the mind receded and I did begin to see the truth as it was available and readily laid before me. And then, I did finally know and for myself realize the truth of what had been always said of the heart being the key. And as my practice and facility continued, I did begin to see a greater and greater amount of light and love entering into me, until my heart was filled to bursting with the love of the Sugmad, and with my desire to share it with all who would listen to my words or feel of my heart and the truth that I had found.

And so, to those who aspire to spiritual greatness, this I do say to you. Return always to your heart, for the wisdom does lie there that shall guide you in your cause, and set you free from pain, and bring you to the very gardens of God-Realization and more, as the heavens do open to you and invite you into their embrace.

The search for spiritual freedom was a long and arduous one, and was not won with power or mental machinations. And so, I did write this poem, that I never would forget the key to seeking of the greatest truth, where it lies hidden beneath.

Prayer for Seekers of the Heart

"The way is long and treacherous,
The road well curved and worn.
Yet never shall you find it,
The greatness you have sworn.
For it is so well hidden,
And never shall be revealed.
Unless you truly are given,
The key to move the stone.
I long have journeyed and stumbled,
Along the dusty road.
But never was I given,
The wine to slake my thirst.
Until I did discern,
The secret that was hidden,
Beneath my very chin.
For the key to certain greatness,
Is not in lines of prose,
Or mental games,
Or clever tricks,
Or power over kingdoms.
It is secreted and hidden,
Beneath the garland rose.
That blooms eternal beauty,
And always does it grow.
Within the heart of champions,
And those who travel home.
And open of their hearts,
To the greatness and are shown.
The secret key to finding,
The sacred Rosetta stone.
That shall guide them in their fortunes,
And never leave them poor,
Or bereft of the love of God.
For the heart is what is given,
To aid all seekers home.
And it must be loved and opened,
If truth is to be won.
For this is the only way,
That God may welcome you home,
And into Its heart above."

This shall be the poem of remembrance and inspiration for all true seekers on the path.

Sri Lai Tsi (spoken directly and verbatim)

The consciousness of the heart is a complex and varied subject that does require great study and perseverance to fully know its ways. And many have come to my temple upon the Mental Plane to hear the truth of what I have learned to aid others on their way. And so, of the heart consciousness and its relationship to reality I can say this.

The heart is the most powerful organ in the body not only from a physical sense, but etherically as a subtle energy center, as well. It is the organ which pumps life giving oxygen to the cells of the body, but, as well, it does channel and bring the prana from the ethers to sustain the living man, and this is how breatharians and others are able to survive without physical sustenance, for they have learned the way and the method to bring the subtle into the material, and through the heart to bring the nourishment via energetic pathways that the physical cells do need. And so, as this life current and energy does enter through the heart to sustain the life of man, so too does it bring with it the coded vibration and information that does give the lower selves their direction and their guidance as to what is the proper way and means of acting to succeed with the best-laid plans of the higher self and Sugmad. For if the direction of the mental or lower bodies is taken, as often is the case when the heart is closed in daily living and decisions made in haste, then certain disaster will befall the Soul in terms of greater illusion and delays upon the path.

However, when the heart is opened and clear, then information from the higher aspect is coded with the energy stream, and in this way can the Soul, of higher perspective and vision, truly guide the lower self in its decisions and its ways. And for this reason is the answer to difficult questions often found during sleep, for this is when the mind does rest and the heart is free to speak and try to lead man on the proper course.

And so, it readily can be seen that the degree of openness of the heart, and clarity of its reception, directly does affect the reality that is created for the Soul upon the path and all decisions that are made as the home of God is sought.

The phrase, "The history of The Way of Truth has been written in the blood of all men," does mean this. Throughout all time those with clear hearts and eyes have fought against the oppression and cruelty of those controlled by the mind, for the mind does always seek to destroy what does threaten it most. And the power of love and of the heart, and the wisdom and truth that is found there, is the greatest threat of all to those who seek by power and fear to maintain what they have achieved. And so, many men have been tortured in ignorance, suppressed and discredited by orthodox religions for the truth that they did bring of personal freedom and liberation, from the yoke that they did bear of the power and tyranny of those in orthodox religions who used the teachings to their own ends.

And though those Souls did not all know the name and origin of the teachings that they had discovered and been given, they had truly learned the freedom that could be won through the wisdom of the heart. And so, throughout the ages men have died and burned for the love they bore their fellow man, and the malice they bore none, save for the great truth they sought to teach to any who would listen. And this is the legacy and heritage and price that have been paid to carry on the works of Spirit.

(End of Sri Lai Tsi's discussion.)

Leytor (spoken directly and verbatim)

The many secrets of the heart here have been given to aid the seeker on, and he would be well to study of their ways and always keep them close to aid him in his difficulties and troubles. However, one last thing does remain to be said. The most efficient means of learning and gathering of great wisdom within the Soul that yearns is the heart–to–heart transmission from the Master in the highest realms, for so many of the secrets and wisdom are beyond the scope of words; and so, it is this method that is preferred by those of greatest accomplishment within the higher planes.

And this is why such prominence and urgency is given to the teachings of the heart, for it is the highest method to learn and speak to any you do encounter when traveling within the higher realms. And so, when you do awaken to the beat and truth of your own heart, always imagine the Master standing near to you, and tell him with your heart of the great love and thanks you bear, and this shall be the greatest way of ever you may act, that shall let the Master and all others know the truth and love you bear within your heart. Of this I shall say no more. Now I am finished.

Chapter Eight

The Path of Least Resistance

That The Way of Truth is "The Path of Least Resistance" does mean the following: Within The Way of Truth, one does learn the many truths and secrets and techniques to opening of the heart and clearing and quieting the mind and allowing the love and truth and power of God to flow through in a balanced and neutral and detached state; for when either the positive or the negative perspective is adopted, this is a state that by its very nature involves or includes a position of resistance to the other; for outside of the neutral state, no position to the left or the right can exist without its counterpart, for this is the Law of Duality and Balance and always must occur. However, the way of love of the heart and the purity and clarity that is gained by attuning the subtle bodies to the frequency and vibration of the HU is the neutral detached state, and like a car on a freeway, when the motor is not engaged, or in neutral, there is no internal resistance to forward motion and progress.

And so, The Way of Truth is the path that teaches the student to find the detached loving state in all matters, to see the truth in life, and this neutral state is the state where the resistance to what comes and must be experienced and overcome is least, and in this way progress is made most swiftly and directly along the path, for any resistance to the left or to the right does only delay the student in the wisdom he must gain and the tests that he must pass to finally finish off his karma and escape the Wheel of 84. And so, The Way of Truth is the path of least resistance when its teachings are learned and adhered, and this shall be the way for greatest progress to be made upon the path and the return to Sugmad's arms.

The physical universe is a contradictory paradox and unity of opposites. Although this does seem a strange thing to the student of The Way of Truth and other paths, it is the nature of this and the lower planes and is so for a very specific reason. To learn to walk and act and exist in the neutral or middle state, then the seeker has first to see and know and understand the nature of those to the left and to the right, for within the upper worlds above the Great Divide, all three states, positive, neutral, and negative, exist and are combined as one. And if the Soul is not facile with its own power and abilities as it does regard these powers, then chaos can be created and no good end would come. And so, the perfection and unity of the higher realms is mirrored down below, but the streams of energy are split to limit their power and destructiveness, so that the Soul can learn its lessons in a controlled and manageable way.

And so, in the physical universe there are three streams of energy and lines of power split from the one above, and although these streams exist independently, they are unified as pairs of opposites to teach the student lessons of the ways of its own home and nature and abilities, which shall be needed up above, for when any action is taken in the higher worlds, it must be taken and done in complete balance of the three forces. So, any creation made by a Soul above the Great Divide does have included in it the elements of sustenance and destruction, as well, in perfect balance and harmony, to keep all things in check and moving and evolving in a harmonious and balanced way.

And so, in the physical and lower worlds are actions and deeds conducted in paired opposites of unity, that when any Soul does create any action from a position too far to the left or right, then there is created karma or some opposite effect to keep the balance the Soul had failed to maintain and to teach it how to see and know and act in a way that is consistent with the skills that it must have to return and live in realms above. And so, it is the challenge of the student to find the middle path and to do all actions in a detached and balanced fashion, that in its deeds and ways the unity of opposites is within contained and held by the power exerted and wielded through the neutral, detached state, for this is the key to escape from the Wheel of 84, though this often does seem a

120

contradictory and confusing thing for the student on the path, for why would it be wise to create a world and way where every opposite is paired with its other in an invisible and unseen way? Would not it be easier to simply open up the gates and let all Souls have their experiences in whatever fashion they desire? But this is not the case, for the Physical Plane is still part of this universe, and all must exist and be maintained in harmony with all others, and without this unity of duality, all could not be maintained within the physical or other realms. And so, though the notion does seem contradictory and strange, it is true that within this plane of God nothing can be made or done without its opposite combined and unified in some unseen way, and these are the lessons of karma and balance that must be learned and obeyed by all upon the path and within this universe.

Negativity is a state of being or an action by one who has moved to the left of the neutral or detached state, and as this one does project its frequency and vibration toward another, it must find the opposite of itself to attach and connect and fulfill its balanced unity. And so, it does require the participation of the other to succeed, for if the receiver does maintain a neutral state, then the negativity must return to its originator to complete itself and find its unified whole, as the Law of Balance within the universe does dictate.

Now, it is not to be confused that the counterpart to negativity, in terms of unified opposites, is necessarily positivity, though this may be the case. In this instance, when negativity is directed toward another, then the unity of opposites that is sought to complete the act being done is a positive projected action of the same negativity that was originally issued to complete the cycle it has created. And so, though it may seem confusing, the act of negative participation on the part of the receiver is a positive act of creation to engage the negativity being received. And this is the key that is sought when this is the circumstance experienced.

Now, when the receiver is neutral and maintains the detached state, then the negativity is returned to the sender, and there it does remain and is held and seeks a similar positive expression of itself from some other Soul within the reality of the one who had originally issued it. And this may not be found for a period of days or weeks; and so, when the negativity is finally returned to the initiator, he may not even know or recall why it is that he has received the negativity from another, for most men are still asleep to the cause and effect of their actions taken from within the imbalanced state. And so, the key to neutral living and freedom from attack or repercussions is to not fall out of balance or send to others in your space feelings or thoughts of a negative or charged manner, for if they are not connected and received they shall return to you and be experienced by yourself at some later time and place. And the same is true for expressions of positivity and warmth but in the expression of its own true self, as well.

Paulji (spoken directly and verbatim)

The statement that "The God-power has a foundation of non-power in the physical realms" can be explained and understood in the following manner. The God-power is the pure energy and power of beingness that is channeled down through the planes and has as its source the Ocean of Love and Mercy, and above the Great Divide, this power comes down through the Lords and Masters of each plane, in different levels of fineness and purity, until it reaches the Etheric Plane, which is just on the south side of the Great Divide. And here this pure unified God-power becomes differentiated into the three streams that are used to build and maintain and create the planes of existence below it.

And so, when a Soul, as man, is within the Physical Plane, his desires and goal should be to learn to access and wield the God-power to do the things and events that comprise his day and interactions with others. However, there isn't any way for the God-power to exist in the physical world because that is not the nature of this plane. And so, the God-power can only be expressed through the heart as the action of neutrality, or detachment, or non-power, for when the student does go with love in his heart and acts and walks from a place of detached goodwill and compassion, then what he is doing is acting as a conduit for the expression of the God-power within the physical world. And what this means is that through the heart, the wisdom and power of the God worlds is able to make itself felt and known. And so, it polarizes the reality of the

122

student and the events around him so that whatever happens and occurs is comprised of the three split streams of energy, but in a recombined and balanced fashion, like it occurs in the God worlds above.

And so, though the actual God-power is not presented in the Physical Plane, the semblance and likeness and similarity of the expression of the God-power are recreated here below, through the power of the heart. Now this is all a somewhat complicated matter, but it's best to think of it like this. When you take any action or look to see for any understanding by using a detached and loving state of neutrality and balance within the heart, then you are using the physical expression of the God-power through the non-action of your ego or lower bodies. And in this way, you will make the decisions and create the actions that are consistent with karma-less creation and further progress on the path.

When I said that, "whatever we are seeking is already here with us, and we don't need to move to the left or to the right," this is what I meant. We are walking Souls who move along the timeline of our experience based on the speed and facility with which we pass the lessons we came here to experience. And many of our deepest desires are for those things that we intuitively know we have set up for ourselves before we came to this incarnation, or if it is not something that we have already set up, it is something that readily can be created out of the use of the imaginative facility. However, the full use of the powers of manifestation, and also of the ability to rapidly move along the experience track, does rely on our ability to maintain the neutral position and not move to the left or right in reaction or positive action away or toward the perceived need to do, for by neutral non-action and detachment, all that is conceived and imagined and known in the higher self does naturally come to us through the polarization of the lower bodies and the reality that is created through them.

And so, everything that we are seeking is typically things that we think will bring us happiness or joy. However, the only happiness that is sustainable is the love of the Sugmad and the joy that is felt when the heart is opened, and that reality becomes known to the seeker on the path because the end result and root cause of all

123

seeking and desire is the desire for love, and the love of the Sugmad is already here with you, but you have to learn how to access it to find the way to bring it into you. And any actions to the left or right are only the ego and lower bodies directing you to action to pursue some illusion or another that takes you farther from the truth of the one way home. And so, the important thing to remember is that, while on the beginning legs of the journey, the key to all you desire is already with you and in the love of your heart. And once you have scaled the heights and become your own master of all you experience and do, then at this point, the key to all you desire is the neutrality of the heart, and the access to the God-power and imaginative facility of the higher bodies above, which shall manifest for you all that you desire and already have in the limitless potential for creation that is the result of the God-power from above.

That the Holy Spirit and Truth are one is a complicated thing to understand, especially as it does relate to being held by power and being dismissed. First, there is this. The Holy Spirit is the voice of Sugmad. The Sugmad is the Ocean of Love and Mercy. The Ocean of Love and Mercy is Truth. So, the Holy Spirit and Truth, therefore, are one. Of this, it is easy to see and understand.

Now, within this universe, there are two types of power: the Kal-power, which is the dual power below the Great Divide, and the God-power, which is the true power in the unified worlds above. Now, the Holy Spirit is Truth and the power of the Holy Spirit is the God-power and is the essence and voice of Sugmad, and hence the true power of the universe. The Kal-power is power, as well, and able to create, sustain and destroy, but it is used for the creation, sustenance and destruction of illusion and not truth or love. And so, within the lower realms, it is the challenge of the student to learn to distinguish between the two. The illusory power of Kal is negative and positive on the one hand, and the true power of the Holy Spirit, of Truth, on the other.

Now, the real complication arises when a Soul seeks to either hold the power of the Holy Spirit as personal power or dismiss it as non-effective or non-existent, for both of these are grave mistakes. The power of the Holy Spirit or Truth serves only Sugmad. It

124

cannot be wielded or controlled for individual purposes or desires by any living Soul. It may be utilized by the co-workers with the Sugmad to do Its will and ways, but Truth and pure God-power can never be utilized for personal ends by a Soul within this universe. And neither may it be dismissed as non-existent or unnecessary or ineffectual, for this is to raise the voice against Sugmad Itself, and this does create negative repercussions of the most severe degree. And so, for the one who believes only and completely in the things and powers of the lower negative worlds, he is preparing himself for a rather unenjoyable experience in this lifetime or after he drops the shell to move on to other realms, for the Sugmad via the Holy Spirit will ensure that that Soul has an experience that will open its eyes to the truth of its ignorant ways as to never repeat the error again. And so, in this way can the Holy Spirit be known as the Truth and the true power in this universe and may not be wielded or dismissed by any who seek to further of his own interests or desires and not of the Sugmad's.

The divine presence exists in each and every one of us and only waits to be awakened and recognized by shifting the perception of our consciousness to the inner and from the outer self. Typically, man looks for his explanations of events and occurrences in terms of outer mechanisms. But this is not the case, for everything that happens on the outer is but a reflection of and result from what has gone before in higher realms. No action in the Physical Plane is without a root cause high above within the inner worlds.

And so, there exists within each one of us the divine presence of Sugmad, but when the attention is placed on outer things, the inner voice is not heard and the power and wisdom and truth of higher realms falls upon deaf ears. And so, as the student begins to learn to quiet of his mind and lower bodies and gradually shift his awareness and focus to the state of detachment and love, then is the divinity inside recognized and awakened and brought from its gentle rest to a manifested position of power and leadership within the affairs of man. And, thus can it be known and seen and experienced by all that the divinity of God is always present inside; it is just to the seeker to find the place to look and quiet of outside disturbances to hear the gentle call and voice of truth that lives within his breast.

Contemplation or the stillness of the mind is the technique used by participants in The Way of Truth and others to open the heart connection to the higher self and through non-action, bring the power, wisdom and truth of higher realms into the Physical Plane. This does polarize the lower bodies and reality of the seeker, as has been said before, to effortlessly create the reality that is in accordance and agreement with the Life Contract of each Soul. The spiritual goals of each student are laid out before the shell is taken, by agreement designed and approved with the Lords of Karma to aid the seeker on the path. And in the case of participants in The Way of Truth, there has been an agreement made to accelerate this process and quickly burn all karma off, that self-mastery and realization might be achieved and the student might then become the artist and master of all he does encounter.

And so, in the first half of this process, the contemplative action does clear the energetic fields of the seeker and quickly draw to him the karmic patterns and conditions he does need to quickly pay his debts. And the stillness of his heart opens the doorway to higher wisdom and the expression of the divine will and plan. And so, the Life Contract is activated and observed and the seeker finds himself in a variety of situations that bring to him the chances and opportunities to resolve the various things that must be done to finally quit the Wheel of 84. And for the seeker who is still in the phase of paying back his debts, this is the purpose and power of contemplation.

Once the seeker has repaid all past life and seed karma, then only daily karma remains, and it is a simple thing to repay and settle this in daily life and living. And for the Soul at this stage, contemplation does begin to take a new meaning and purpose and function. For the one who has fulfilled the conditions of his life karma and contract now does have the opportunity to begin to create the life that is desired through the spiritual tools of Spirit and techniques of manifestation. And as long as what is sought is not directly in violation with any previous agreements or prohibitions, the Soul is free to do as it does please, as long as the balanced state is maintained and adhered to.

And for those at this stage, contemplation is the way that the higher self is contacted and the powers there are reached and accessed to create what is desired, as long as it is in harmony with Spirit and is done in a way that serves the highest good for all involved, for one cannot simply wish for riches and a life of ease just because all past debts have been paid. These are things that easily can be had and won, but must be done in a way of service to the Holy Spirit and other Souls and in support of best-laid plans of the Sugmad and other hierarchies.

And so, the test of learning to use the tools of mastery is finding ways and means to combine your desires and wishes and blend them with the Holy Spirit, in a neutral and balanced way that keeps you free of karma; receive the things you need and desire in the way that you do wish, for the ladder of understanding and proficiency always has another rung, and the challenges and fruits of each step are the bittersweet victory for the hard-won knowledge and pain that is experienced and received at each step along the way.

The passive state of consciousness can be used when the student is still trying to open his heart and energetic bodies to the flow of God-power to bring to him those situations which are next to be experienced along the course and path of his development. But within each act of passive manifestation, of karma or some other situation for resolution or that is desired, there is an active element as well which is required to complete the cycle of action and occurrence. So, for example, when a specific action is brought into your reality through contemplation to draw that lesson to you, this is a passive action, for it was brought into your reality by the Holy Spirit to give to you the opportunity to resolve the outstanding issue and move along the path. However, it does require an active spiritual and consciousness movement to complete the cycle that was originally created; and so, this is the dual nature and lesson of the skill and act of contemplation.

For the student must learn to see and know when to be passive and allow the experience to come, and when to be active, to engage and complete the cycle that has been begun, and a good way to tell what to do is this: When the circumstance or action does arise out

127

of what might seem coincidence, this is an example of the passive act at play and utilizing and expressing the God-power from above. And when this coincidental situation does arise, this is a key that now active action is required to complete what has been begun and allow the passive to then bring to you the next experience, which is required to aid you on your way.

Now, when this does really get tricky is when the experiences begin to overlay and overlap, and then it does take true wisdom of the heart and keen observance to see and clearly know which is which and what is the proper action and course that you should take. But, above all, the thing to remember is this: The passive state of consciousness is that in which the Holy Spirit works through you to bring something to your side. The active state is when you do join and blend your energies with it to complete the task at hand and do what must be done or achieve what must be gained. And this is the skill and ability that those students on the path must learn and master to finally return back home to God and the Ocean of Love and Mercy up above.

When I did say, "It is God who works and not you," I did mean the following: All that is achieved in life is through the wielding of the God-power. When it is wielded by one of higher awareness and from the unified state, it creates and acts in a balanced fashion, as it would from up above, and this is its signature within the lower worlds. But the power of the Kal, the divided streams, is God-power, as well, just in a different form. And so, when it is said that all creation is from God, this is technically true. Although the awakened and wise student on the path does know that if he is open and has love in his heart, he is able to serve as a conduit and as a co-worker with this creation from above, and this is the goal and destiny of every Soul within the many universes of the great Father above.

The possession of the balance required to bring the God-power into life will begin to affect and change the life of the seeker and of all those around him in subtle but powerful ways. The most immediate effect to be seen will be the changing of friends and acquaintances, as those who are incompatible with the new vibration and frequency or those whose Life Contracts or realities do not mesh with that of the seeker are begun to be moved away that others may come in who are in greater alignment and coherence with the new state of awareness of the student. And, as well, will some physical changes be seen as old infirmities do slip away or changes in weight may be seen, or eyesight, or hair or appearance of aging and youth. All these things and more may be seen when the God-power does begin to flow, because the God-power is a force of such purity that no darkness or negativity can exist within proximity to the one who bears it. And friends and family and close acquaintances who are bound to the one by bonds of love do receive of some of this power, as well; and so, their lives and persons shall too begin to change in subtle but powerful ways. And often these changes shall be for the better, but some shall sense the light and the power and shall be afraid and shall run. And so, some friendships or co-workers or family members may be lost or estranged, as they do move on and seek others closer to their own awareness and unfoldment. And this is not a negative thing but something that must merely be seen and understood and accepted, for none can force another to his place and level, and the mark of a true Master and one well advanced on the path is the compassion to allow another the grace to carry on and proceed at his own pace and level of comfort. And so, these may be some of the changes that are seen in the possessor of the God-power and those who are close to him.

Now, the application of the non-power in a balanced way is truly the art to be learned and mastered, if one is to find and have the life that is desired within the Physical Plane, and the way to use the non-power of the God-power is to quietly go within and see the things that you do desire in your heart and to see them as an outcome and not as a thing in action or a cause to get you to the place you do desire to be, for the trick to using the non-power in a balanced way is to envision of the end goal and then let the Holy Spirit and the Lords of Karma decide what is the way to get you to the place you want to be without creating or incurring any karma along the way. And so, this is one way to use the non-power with balance to achieve the ends you want.

The second way is to follow the gentle nudges and urges of your heart and higher self and see where they do lead, for if you are following the path and destiny and life mission that has been laid out for you, then when you do proceed in a balanced and detached state, the doors shall all begin to open, as if by magic and hands unseen, and all that must be done to achieve greatness and glory in your deeds along the path is to do as you do see the way, but with a detached heart and never wavering to the left or to the right, for the gifts of Spirit are limitless and have no end or final point but are only slowed or impeded by the clouding of your own heart and the influence you allow by the negative power and the action of the Kal. And so, in this second instance, you must learn to see and follow the Golden Trail that is laid before you, to guide you on your way. And if you do fulfill what is needed in a detached and loving way, then you shall have all the riches that are yours as a result and balanced response to the great love and gifts you give. And so, these are just two ways to use of the non-power in a balanced way to achieve the goals and desires of your heart and mission.

(End of Paulji's dialogue.)

Agnotti (spoken directly and verbatim)

The difficulties of life may be transcended by folding time and space to overcome all obstacles and challenges encountered on the path. But how can this be done? It sounds a miraculous thing that is only the way of Masters and saviors and others of tremendous spiritual merit. The answer lies in our understanding of the dynamics of what is occurring, and the techniques that may be learned and applied to utilize these facts of wisdom and understanding.

Challenges in the student's life arise for only two reasons. First, to teach a lesson or repay a karmic debt that is part of the Life Contract and agreement made by the student and agreed to with the Lords of Karma. This is the type of thing that occurs when a student is moving along the path and burning large amounts of karma in an effort to rid himself of all burdens and escape the Wheel of 84. The second reason why difficulties may be encountered is that the Soul is taking action that goes against the will of the Sugmad and Its wishes and desires as to how Its power is used and wielded by the one below to achieve of best-laid plans. And so, these are the two types of challenges and difficulties that are predominantly encountered.

Now, in the first instance where it is a karmic situation, then the means of folding time and space to transcend the problem is a simple matter. What the student does seek to achieve is an understanding of the problem and a way to rearrange the engrams that have created and contributed to the situation in a way that all, or nearly all, of the energy is resolved and cleared and dissipated within the inner realms and beyond the physical world of time, space, energy and matter. And so, the process to fold time / space and accelerate the resolution of the matter is this. First, the student must gain an understanding of the root cause and effect of the situation. To do this, he may use one of several techniques, however, the method I prefer is to go to Shamus i Tabriz at the temple where he works and watches over the Soul records of each individual, and ask, what is the reason and root cause of the difficulty, which has been encountered? And if one is successful in this effort, he will then be shown, or will later realize in a dream or in an experience with the Wisdom of the Masters, the answer he does seek. This is the first step of the process, to understand why things are as they have become.

The second step is to ascertain if anything may be done to shift the circumstances which have occurred, and if so, what? This may be done by going to the Lords of Karma and humbly standing before them and asking them these things. One, may this karma be shifted or dissolved, or does it have to be experienced? And, two, what can be done within the inner realms, and beyond time and space, to resolve the situation beyond the Physical Plane? If the answer to the first question is yes, then the student must then return to Shamus i Tabriz or some other Master who teaches and watches over them, to receive a technique that may be used to resolve the matter at hand, for the situation manifested on Earth is merely the effect of causes high above, and the student adept at spiritual skills can learn to see and change the conditions which created the physical difficulty, without having to even leave his home or favorite place of contemplation.

131

A word of caution is here given though, to be patient in your efforts and expectations, for once the course of remedy is invoked there is always a time of delay between the action and the physical manifestation down below because of the effect of free will and man's own individual decisions and choices. So be patient and be steadfast in your commitment and all shall proceed as you do desire.

Now for difficulties arising from a crossing of the will of the Sugmad, this is a different matter. And if Shamus i Tabriz does say that no karma is being enacted, then one can assume that merely a direction and action of life has been taken that is not in agreement with the intended use of the power that has been given. And in these instances, the student must learn to go within and ask for more direction as to what is the proper way and course of action to bring alignment back and all efforts in a way that does support of best-laid plans. Though these might seem of difficult ways to discern and resolve all things, with practice, the student shall, over time, gain the facility and skill to judge between the two and quickly seek the answers to resolve the challenges faced in a means that is efficient and transcends time and space and returns the student quickly to the Holy Spirit far above.

The universal consciousness is the collective consciousness of all that exists within this universe, not just on Earth, but on all planets, in all galaxies from within all the worlds of the Sugmad. And so, as a Soul, as an individual unit of consciousness within the lower five planes, it is the function and responsibility of the universal mind consciousness to send its wisdom and knowledge to those it knows below, for all thoughts, which it is, are created and stored in the Mental Plane below the Great Divide, and to which it is attached to each and every Soul that still maintains bodies in the planes below the Soul.

And so, it is the job and function to make all knowledge known and available to all within its realms. And the mental body of each Soul is constantly flooded with thoughts, as the universal mind consciousness does seek to do its job and share what it does know. And this is why you do see such a variety of creative works that portray events and people and species of far off places, for this is just the mental body opening to and receiving the information that has been contributed in some far off land or place, that each Soul and species upon the Earth might someday come to realize the unity of itself and its destiny with all others, and hasten to its home in the Holy Spirit far above. And so, for this reason and purpose, the universal mind consciousness does exist to aid the cause of all Souls by showing what is learned between the various peoples and planets and galaxies to aid each on their way and in their great return.

Each Soul that walks the Earth does serve as a part and member of some Hierarchy within the inner realms. For without this Order and Hierarchy, there would be chaos and no control and all would soon cease to function or exist. And so, within the Hierarchy or Order that is served, each Soul is assigned another, an Oversoul, or as Christians would refer, a guardian angel, to watch over the Soul in its charge and see that its development and course of actions comply with its duties above and what must be done to maintain of order and functioning within the world below. And so, too, do these Oversouls join together to coordinate of events, relationships, occupations, communications and all other types of occurrence and manifestation within the planes below.

When Soul awakens and begins to take responsibility for itself, it can be given higher spiritual duties. This decision is made by the Living Sehaji Master who cooperates with Milarepa and the Grand Council as to Soul's assignment and development of its present spiritual skills. This type of Soul assignment is unique and further reviewed by the Silent Nine. This type of dharma is rarely given by the Living Sehaji Master and is an acknowledgment of the Soul's humility and commitment to best laid plans.

So when you do seek through contemplation to resolve of a situation or event through the use of inner means, you must first consult and obtain the permission of the Oversoul who does watch over any other with which you do seek to affect. The exception to this rule is when you do bring the other Soul into the light of the Living Sehaji Master, for then it is the responsibility of the Holy Spirit to manage the situation and the other hierarchies involved and they will understand and any transgressions shall be forgiven.

But in any other case, the Oversoul must first be consulted and its permission granted for any action taken, which may affect the other or the circle of its reality or place. For this is why many psychics do often find themselves in peril, for they have violated the agreements and situations put in place by those above, without first consulting or asking permission of the ones that they do serve. And so, each student should not make the mistake of merely seeing physical occurrences as phenomena of only this plane, but should peer behind the curtain to see what does remain hidden and does guide with unseen hands.

To speak to, or obtain permission from, one who does watch over another, you can in contemplation see the one you know and then behind his head, as if floating on a tether, you may see the one that is known as the Oversoul. And to this one, you must ask your questions and request what you seek to do. If you do not see any cord or another attached, then you must place the one you are seeking within the blue light of the Living Sehaji Master's love, and say to that Soul, "I do not seek to interfere with the plans of any other. I offer the love of the Living Sehaji Master as proof of my good intention and wish only to send love." And in this way shall any error be corrected automatically and the student shall be protected from the harm of his ignorance or inability.

Non-resistance to the flow of life, of the God-power, is the key to all success. And resistance comes from out of balance reactions by the lower bodies of man that create disturbances and darkness that slows the flow of love and power from within the higher realms. And so, the key and the desire of each student should be to learn to view all events from a detached perspective and maintain the neutral state, which the God-power should swiftly and easily flow through you in an unimpeded way. And the key to gaining this detached perspective and state is in raising the consciousness and gaining the ability to see the root cause and energy of all events and things, and in this way the understanding may set the student free. For ignorance and fear are the roots of attachment. And understanding and love are the things that dissolve and destroy ignorance and fear. And this is the way that the detached state is won and achieved, and the flow of God-power opened, increased and maintained. And so, through raising of the consciousness may all other things be obtained and greatness and glory won, as is the destiny and right of man.

The attitude of the seeker is a very important thing, for it is the conscious decision which does polarize the lower bodies and affect the center of the heart and how much love is received and given to aid of best-laid plans, for the attitude is a conscious reality choice that does affect of all experiences that the student truly has. And a negative attitude does polarize the energy field with negativity and attracts those things to it that do portray the negative portion of the experience pair of unity that must be manifested and dealt with. For each karmic or other experience that the student does manifest to learn and burn the karma it has sown is comprised of a negative and positive counterpart. And either end may still fulfill the obligation of the mission or Life Contract or experience that must be had, yet, often the attitude of the seeker does affect which one is presented into the personal reality of the one who has the lesson to learn.

And so, a positive attitude not only brings those things closer to you and at a more rapid pace that do bring love and happiness in life, but can also affect, to a degree, how karmic events are brought and structured and experienced and paid along the way of resolving all balances still existing upon the Wheel of 84. So, the important thing to remember is always to adopt, no matter how difficult it is, a positive attitude and lightness of heart. For in this way shall your lessons be as painless as they possibly can, but also shall speed to you the good things of this life that you desire and deserve to succeed along the path.

Once the consciousness is raised above the worlds of materiality, then no one is able to hurt you and karma only exists as much as you give power to it. Though this is a strange sounding thing to say, it is truth once it is understood, for the ability of someone to hurt you is governed by first the Law of Karma, and, second by our willingness to move out of neutrality and engage with the one whom oppresses us and seeks to do us harm. And by our movement out of non-power and into Kal-power, or to the left or the right, this does give to the other the foothold to connect his energy to ours and in this way do us harm. But if our consciousness does exist and is focused and remains beyond the planes of materiality, then we are in a constant state of balance and far beyond the place where our enemy can engage us and bring harm to our way. For remember, no action within the physical realm can exist without its counterpart above; and so, when the position of non-power is assumed within the heart and consciousness, then no lower world connection is possible within the dual planes, and so, no harm may be done to us.

As for the Law of Karma, when we do exist and have found a home within the worlds above and beyond the realms of materiality, then all actions we do take are done in a balanced and neutral and karmically free way. And so, the only way the Law of Karma can be enacted and brought to bear its weight is if we do decide consciously to move far to the left or right, and so, allow the law to engage to balance what we have done and create the debt to be paid. But when we are situated in the elevated consciousness, this does become a choice and an option for the Soul to make, for no longer are all deeds done in ignorance of the law and ways and what is the proper way.

Within the realm of non-power, illusion cannot exist, for it is a thing and manifestation of only the lower worlds, and the pure God-power, which does comprise the non-power, is sent from far above in the worlds of pure beingness and love. And so, the only way for illusion to exist is by the exercise of the Kal-power, and the Kal-power only may be used for creation and destruction by those who are ignorant of the ways of the non-power to act in balanced ways to create in the fashion of the Gods without illusion or pain or the sense of reality that is tried when illusion does set in. And so, for those who trod along the path and do wish to avoid of illusion and Maya, keep your hearts open and detached and the flow of the non-power alive, for this is the best way to be sure that you do step neither to the left nor the right and all illusion and Maya are kept below and not allowed to achieve a grip or hold on you or slow you on your way and your journey on the path.

(End of Agnotti's dialogue.)

Absolute neutrality is the goal of every student to allow the non-power of the God-power to enter his heart and work through him. But to accomplish of this goal is no easy matter, for it is like standing on the top of the highest mast of the ancient sea-going schooners, and telling the winds of a mighty tropical storm to stay their lashing tongues. Yet, it is the goal and task that must be done, if the student is to succeed in his endeavors on the path within this physical world, for absolute neutrality is that place where the tumultuous winds of the lower bodies are stilled and the golden radiance and love of the sun of God can shine through to warm the hearts of all men.

And so, to achieve this desired state, the student must constantly evaluate the nature of all events that are presented within his reality and seek to know their root cause and purpose, and then with this understanding may any ripple or disturbance from the left or from the right be counterbalanced and cancelled out and no distraction shall be felt, for any predilection or variance in the heart to either the left or the right, to repulsion or attraction, shall be the thing that does cause the neutrality to be lost. For the battle within man, and that he does always face, although it does grow easier with time and experience, is to tame the mighty winds of illusion and Maya, which do buffet him from either side, for these are the ways that Souls are made strong and prepared for greater battles.

So, the anxious student on the path should pursue the spiritual exercises he is given with diligence and a good attitude and open heart, for these are the training programs designed for Soul to slowly but expeditiously and directly open the heart and begin the disciplining and focus and control of the lower bodies, for the body and heart and reflexes of the mighty warrior samurai of old were not trained in the fields of lilies and milk and honey, but against the wet, dark nights and the discipline and cold of harshest conditions where Soul's mettle is surely known. And so, with discipline and persistence will the glories of God be won and the training of the lower bodies achieved and the absolute neutrality desired be finally brought to bear.

Spiritual freedom is that state that the enlightened Soul finds itself in when it is no longer buffeted and tossed about by the winds of illusion and change but is like the calm in the eye of the hurricane where tranquility and love do rule, but within the mighty tempest of everyday life and living. And it is within this place of sanctuary and refuge that the Soul does find itself beyond the realm of good and evil, for good and evil are only two labels that can be applied to those things that either aid or hinder man on his journey of understanding and unfoldment. And so, in this state the directive to "resist not evil" does take on a new significance and meaning, for to resist the negativity of the Kal does mean to move to left of center and give to illusion some foothold to grasp and cling to you and in this way participate in its desires to lead you astray. But if absolute neutrality is maintained, then the evil does have no foothold to gain and must return to whence from it was sent. And so, this is the meaning and the wisdom behind the phrase "resist not evil" as the answer and the way to succeed upon the path and move on to higher realms.

When the student finally has begun to open of the heart to the flow of love and non-power, the Holy Spirit shall begin to present to it opportunities to do its will and way and serve of its desire to spread the news of its wisdom and its love through the teachings of The Way of Truth and the love and truth of the Living Sehaji Master. And so, for the student to find and do what must be done, the following is a good idea to speed along the way, for love given in the service of the Holy Spirit is always received a thousand-fold to the one who gave it so, for the Holy Spirit does watch over and reward its own children, though this never should be the reason or motivation for seeking to serve to give the love to others' hearts.

But as the Holy Spirit does move you to seek avenues of service, the student can go within in contemplation and find the light of the Living Sehaji Master, and from your heart can say to him, "Master, how may I be of service? Lead me to the proper place to tell what must be said, and I shall open my heart to love and bring the word of Spirit." And in this way shall the Holy Spirit in a natural and effortless way bring to the student opportunities to give and serve the love he has found within his own heart and studies. And great merit shall be earned and great progress made upon the path to

138

speed him ever home. There are two kinds of seekers in this world, those that are content to listen to and believe in the experiences of others and those who must have these experiences for themselves. And the students of The Way of Truth are those of the latter disposition, for the special characteristic of the path of The Way of Truth and the protection and guidance of the Master is that each student can and must have his own experiences with the Light and Sound of God, for what good does it do a Soul to find itself in the inner worlds if all he has ever done is read books about the subject but never experienced its power or circumstance with his own heart and faculties?

And so, this is why The Way of Truth is a very effective path for learning the skills and abilities that are needed up above, and receiving the training and wisdom that will enable the Soul to finally see the truth of lower realms and escape the Wheel of 84, for without those direct and personal experiences, he never would be able to ascend to higher realms and know the rules and principles and disciplines of how to conduct himself, and so would fail and be returned to lower realms to try again to learn. And so, this is the special consideration and aspect that is given to the student to aid him on his way and well prepare him for what shall be faced and seen and known when he does enter the worlds above that are his true home and destiny.

There are two basic ways that students in life see and categorize and seek to understand their reality: the extrovertive and the introvertive. Those with extrovertive perceptions do always seek to find the cause and effect relationship within the outer world in already manifested physical reality, while those of the introvertive perception do always seek the inner cause of what did occur and happen. And the former never shall see with clear eyes the true nature of cause and effect, while the latter shall always see and know what to do to carry on and succeed with what is sought, for the answer to all queries of "why" does lie within the inner realms, for no action in the physical world does occur without its counterpart above. And so, for the seeker on the path who does seek to make with haste in the direction of the top of the mountain, this is a good rule and guide of thumb to always be remembered. Use the spiritual tools that have been given to aid you in your cause and in your way. And your sight into the heart of problems, as they do lie within the inner realms, shall be the guiding force to set you clearly on your way and bring to you the success your heart does truly desire, for this is the truth and wisdom of all that you do seek to aid you on your path and in your way.

The Soul Contract or life mission of the student on the path is a general set of agreements and conditions that do govern the major events and milestones that shall occur in the seeker's lifetime. Though this is agreed and spelled out in general terms, there are instances of more detailed missions and agreements, if that is needed and justified. But, at any rate, this is the way that the Hierarchy and best-laid plans are served, and the Soul does receive the experience that is needed in this life to pay off or receive karmic debts and be confronted with the lessons and tests that are required to successfully complete this life and mission. And so, from the very start, the type of life the student will have is generally dictated and known, but not always set in stone or taken for granted, for the student who does face and pass his tests without fear or hesitation may quickly find himself at the end of his Life Contract and mission that has been fulfilled, and then the student does have the opportunity to choose. He may either continue to burn additional karma from his reservoir and store, or he may create for himself, in the remaining years he has before it is time to go, the life that is desired according to his interests and passions and desires or the Soul may simply decide to drop its body and leave, as often is the case, especially among those who have repaid a heavy debt and are tired of this shell and of this planet. And so, it is at the discretion of the one as to how he shall choose once his obligations have been fulfilled.

But how can a Soul know if its contract has been completed? In one or several ways: First, the Soul may notice an abrupt shift and change in its life and reality, to include family, work, friends, health, financial status or geography, from what has normally been the pattern and the way. Second, the Soul can go to stand before the Lords of Karma and ask for confirmation of what is suspected or hoped, and it may be received in one of the usual ways: immediately, or in a day or week or so. The third way is to go to the Living Sehaji Master and ask to see and know what is the truth of the situation or if your heart does see things properly and in the clearest way. And so, in one of these ways shall you know and understand the truth of the karmic matter and can evaluate the choices that you do have and make the proper decision.

The Soul Contract can be an element that facilitates or hinders the spiritual development of man, for it does depend on what was decided and arranged before the Soul came in. If the Soul and the Lords of Karma have agreed that this is to be a life of rest and enjoyment, then few challenges and lessons may be provided to spur the seeker on. If, however, the Soul has indicated the desire to rapidly grow and learn, it may be faced with numerous challenges and difficulties to bring to it the tests and circumstances of learning that it does desire and need to progress rapidly along the path. And in some instances, the contract may be negotiable to some degree, but this is rarely so, for the Lords of Karma do labor carefully to make each contract so, that it does function and serve of best-laid plans to keep all balance met and the universe and collective karma and consciousness proceeding at a pace and in a way that is best for all concerned.

One of the laws of this universe is that no Soul is given any problem or challenge that does exceed its ability to learn the lesson and overcome it and triumph and move on, for what truly would be the point of a lesson that could not be learned and succeeded? The Soul would merely become frustrated, or worse, decide to move on and forcibly depart the shell through suicide or some other manner or means. And so, the key element to remember is that all challenges and problems within your reality are created by the polarization of your own energetic bodies to bring to you the lessons that you do need to aid you on your way and in your unfoldment. And how could a reality created by your own self be greater than the thing that in the first place did create it? And so, the key thing to remember and always know is that no matter how difficult the challenges do become, there is always a way and a solution to the problem you do face. The key does lie in the spiritual techniques and exercises that are given and explained here and in other wisdom of The Way of Truth that may be found upon the Earth and within the inner planes.

141

Why is it important to know and understand your mission in life? This would seem a self-evident question, but often it is not, and so, does bear the merit of an answer. The life mission of the student should be known because it does allow the student to contextualize and understand and make sense of the events and people and occurrences that have shaped him and where and who he is, for misunderstanding and ignorance are the roots of illusion and fear; and so, a knowledge of your mission and the role you have agreed to play is a liberating method of bringing harmony of purpose and understanding to your heart. And so, it is wise for the student to expend some time and energy to seek and understand the reason for his life and the opportunity that is laid before him to do what he must do and find the glory and greatness that is his right by birth.

There are several ways to find out and understand what is your mission and contract. The first, and most direct, is to go to Shamus i Tabriz, or to the Lords of Karma, and humbly stand before them and ask what you do wish to know. And depending on the merit and abilities and skill of the student, this may work or it may not. The second way is to go to the Living Sehaji Master in contemplation, or an initiate's report, and ask humbly to be shown what is the mission and purpose and why have you come to Earth. And often you may not receive a direct answer, but things shall begin to shift and move, and over time, the truth and circumstances shall emerge as to what is your mission and destiny.

Now a word of caution is here mentioned. Often, to get you to the place to fulfill your mission and destiny, the Holy Spirit shall have to lead you through various doors to arrive at the destination you do seek. So, do not become frustrated or disheartened if the first thing that does present itself and occur does not turn out to be the one that shall be the final place, for it may take some time and patience and trial and error for all things to finally fall in place. But the practice of neutrality and the non-power of above shall hasten all things to you and bring you to your place and into the mission that you are truly here to fulfill.

This chapter has been devoted to the secrets of the heart and the non-power of the God-power as the means and as the way to bring rapidly to the student the things that must be seen and experienced and overcome to aid him on his way and in his travels. However, the key thing to always remember and know is this: The Way of Truth is a vehicle for combining and presenting of the truth in a coherent and complete fashion, like never has been done before. All religions, theologies, paths, teachings and walks of life have elements of truth and light in varying degrees, for truth is universal and found even within the trees and forests of the most remote lands upon the Earth. And so, in a sense may all these different ways and paths be considered children and family of The Way of Truth, for the truth that each does bear. But The Way of Truth is the Golden Thread that binds them all together in a cohesive and understandable way, for no other significant path upon the Earth contains as much purity and truth and wisdom, in a comprehensive and understandable and relevant fashion, as does the teachings of The Way of Truth. And though all other paths do have merit and their place and are not to be condemned or castigated under any condition or circumstance, The Way of Truth is truly the most rapid way to quickly learn and ascend the top of the mountain and forever leave this Earth and the divided planes below.

Chapter Nine

The Eternal Truths of God

Leytor (spoken directly and verbatim)

The eternal truths of God are those constants throughout the universe that do pertain to the functioning and mechanics of how the upper and lower worlds do work. The truths of God do transcend all teachings, Masters, and paths and are contained and taught by different ways, in differing degrees, by those throughout the ages as was appropriate and relevant to their culture and their times and the state of development of the collective consciousness and reality that was unfolding at that time. And so, when saviors or saints or great teachers have come, it has often been to bring that piece or pieces of universal eternal truth for which his or her followers were ready to take the next step along the path.

As well, there is relative or situational truth, which differs from eternal truth. Relative truth is truth given and learned that pertains only to a specific level of consciousness, and the challenge and test to ascend past that level of consciousness is to peer within and through what is considered the relative truth of that state, to see the falsity of it, and proceed onward to the next level. However, when the student is imbued and struggling to master that level of consciousness and understanding, the relative truth is believed to be eternal truth, and until the discernment is learned and achieved, those who hold the relative truth close to their hearts can be quite adamant and aggressive that theirs is the proper or only way. However, as discernment is mastered and more lessons are learned and the student progresses on the path, the relative truth is seen and known for what it truly is, and the student does progress.

The Way of Truth is comprised only of eternal truth, for this is one of the things that makes it such an efficient and direct path, for no time is wasted or lost chasing the relative truth of lower paths and levels; and so, the student is given the pure truth of the highest realms in a condensed and continuous teaching that expedites the learning and development and release from lower worlds.

There are three types of eternal truth: Soul truth, which does pertain to the Soul and its functioning, abilities and awareness; lower world truth, which does relate to all things of illusion and below the Great Divide; and, higher world truth, which are those truths and laws that do relate to and are a part of the perfection of the higher worlds beyond the realms of matter, energy, space and time. And so, for the student of The Way of Truth, and those of other paths, all truth and understanding can be known and understood within the parameters of this categorical system.

Truth and existence are interwoven and not separate in their nature and very being. Existence depends on truth to tell those who inhabit and perpetuate it of how things function and must be done to keep all cycles moving and the universe alive and breathing and growing, for without truth, existence would be merely a barren wasteland and sea of undifferentiated energy and stillness, and the Sugmad would know nothing, save the calm of Its own heart. And so, truth is how the laws and rules and secrets of creation and all other functions are given to those It loves to teach and guide them in the way that keeps all harmony and balance and fulfills of best-laid plans. And because existence is infinite and unbroken, thus is truth, eternal truth, of the same nature and essence, for it is woven and born of that same thing that it describes and teaches of, and forever shall the two remain combined and inseparable in their content and their nature.

The goal of the student's life is to see beyond the illusion and seek the truth in each and every moment of every life, for the truth is a liberating and energizing seed and ray of light that dispels all darkness and negativity and frees the student from his bonds and speeds him on his way and return to higher realms. And the instrument of the perception and understanding of truth is Soul. So, to seek and find the presence of truth in all your daily efforts and

146

doings, use the techniques of the heart and the HU and the God-power that previously have been described, for these are the ways that the truth may be seen and heard and known to set you free.

Sugmad has as its mission and duty to man to impart Its truths to Its sons and daughters through the Masters and teachings that are sent below to Earth and other places to aid those on the path. And so, the Sehaji have long been the bearers of the eternal universal truth since the very dawn of time. The teachings have not always been called The Way of Truth, for that is the modern name the vehicle has been given to contain the teachings of our Order, yet the Masters have all shared our lineage back to the dawn of time in an unbroken stream of love and wisdom and sharing. And so, for man in his earliest beginnings, in the Hyperborean age and before, when he was just a filmy cloud of life floating on the ethers, the Living Sehaji Masters were there to guide and show the way and help shape of events to do what must be done to gently nudge man on his next step and progression a little farther down the path. And so, the Sehaji have always directly served Sugmad in this way, to bring the highest purest truth and love from the Holy Spirit far above to those upon the Earth who were ready to hear Its words.

The eternal truths of Sugmad remain unchanged throughout the universe and transcend time and place. To different races, species, life forms, times and galaxies and planets, truth remains the same, though told in a different language and through different writings and through examples and descriptions that are culturally relevant to the conditions that do exist. And in many of those places the Living Sehaji Masters do exist in other forms, with other faces and other manners of speech and dress, and they do teach the eternal truths to those who follow them and seek to know the wisdom of their ways.

At some point in the future, there will come a conquering race from distant places that will rule over Earth, and they will practice The Way of Truth, and one of their kind shall come and lead the flock on Earth in the teachings of love and truth and compassion and humility that are taught by the Master, today, for universal eternal truth shall be the thing that binds the human race together and gives to it a common ground and reference of understanding to share with those who come, for it must be understood that eternal truth builds bridges and community, and not the other way, of the destruction and divisiveness of the illusion of the Kal.

So, this is why it is important to study and to learn the skills of discernment and other ways and techniques that are taught within these books, for the time of this occurrence is no longer that far off. And when the day does come, the world shall rely on those who know and understand and embrace eternal truth, for this shall be the way that peace shall be achieved and many lives saved from suffering and unnecessary loss. Those who are blinded by illusion shall experience great pain and suffering, as they are deluded by their lack of wisdom and the dark forces of the Kal, as is its way and job and function.

The initiations in The Way of Truth are designed to bring the student to a higher level of truth and understanding of what is the eternal way and wisdom that shall free him from his bonds and speed his return to higher realms and the golden light above, for the greater amount of God-power that we are given access to in our initiations and achievements is what does determine and govern the amount and level of truth we can perceive and know, for truth, as well, is power and does come with a responsibility to do the proper thing, once it is had and known. And so, as the Soul matures and develops, it is given greater freedom and abilities to see the secrets of God and know the eternal truths that can pierce the veil below, and this is how the student truly progresses on the path.

The Laws of God are many, but for our purposes, here we shall address in detail a few of the most important to aid the student on his way and in his endeavors. The Law of God is the overriding rule and condition that is most important to know, for the Law of God does state that all that exists within this universe is created by Its thought and word; and so, all exist because It loves it, and nothing more is there beyond Its love and all creation. So, the Law of God is meant for faith, when all else does seem to fail you, and for when doubt is encountered on the path or the power of the Kal has seeped into your heart and brought you seeds of mistrust and misgivings, for the Law of God does say that you need only look about at all the wonders and marvels to know that God exists and this is all Its world and Its domain and creation.

The Law of HU is second in nature and importance, for it does pertain to the word of Sugmad's heart and breath; and so, this is important because any who do seek of heavenly realms must know and abide and walk within the truth of the Law of HU. The Law of HU does state that this is the heart and way to ascend the mountain of God with greatest facility and haste and soon find yourself alone at the top of the mountain and with only the love of Sugmad to keep your heart warm and alight with the love of all in existence, for the HU is the key and way that all wisdom may be granted and all power and truth obtained; and so, the Law of HU is the one that truly says that this is the key to unlock the doors of heaven, and all would do well to know and always remember that this is the purest way to quench the burning desire within your heart.

The Law of Soul does say that this is a piece of God and of Its fabric and Itself, and It did create Its children to walk upon the Earth and other planes and places and learn what was Itself and Its nature and Its essence. And all conscious things and beings are Soul, for none can live without it, and none can perceive or be or know without the faculty that it is. And so, the Law of Soul does say that it exists because It loves it, and nothing else there is that matters or can be said of importance to those who understand. This law is important to remember when questions do arise as to the reasons for compassion and the need to give love and warmth to others who may not seem deserving or desirous to receive the hard won truth and feeling that the love of God does give to those cold hearts who walk along the path, so cold and dark and forgotten.

The Law of Love does state that this is the only way and the key by which the heavens may be opened and the truth and wisdom won and brought to light and service within the lower realms. All that exists does so because of love. Love of Sugmad and between all Souls is the fire that fuels the universe and the glue that keeps it together and continuing on its way and evoking and unfolding as all does cycle and continue to move and carry on. Love, though it is greatly misunderstood and maligned for other purposes and meanings, is the only thing that can bring salvation, and is the greatest power of all, if used in the proper way. And so, those who abide the Law of Love will always look for a way to express and utilize this frequency to bring the light of God and Its wisdom to all their endeavors and actions within this plane below.

The Law of Karma does truly say that for each action taken from the left or from the right, there is an equivalent opposite that must be returned and repaid to keep all balance and harmony within the universe of God and to teach the student lessons of how is the proper way to act and wield the many strong and powerful energies of the God worlds above the Great Divide. And so, the Law of Karma, though it is often the most painful, is the greatest balancing principle that guides the life of man and all Souls, as they do struggle along the path and to learn the proper way. And to avoid invoking the Law of Karma, one is wise to know and learn the proper way to take of actions, that any should be done via the non-power of neutrality, and in the certain way that the will and action and desire is blended with the Holy Spirit and resolved in a way such that no ripple or residual effect is created to tie you to the one to whom the action is created.

The Law of Detachment does say that the requirement for success is the detached and loving state in which no troubles do find an urgency and ability to sway you from your course and neutral state, and no passion nor any fear can bring you to your knees or close your heart to the frequency that the non-power does rely to bring the God-power and wisdom into the Physical Plane and other realms below the Great Divide, for the detached state is the key to all understanding, and never should the student be swayed to go to the left or to the right to take of any action or entertain any debate of what is the proper way and course of action, for the only sure way and path is the middle road of detachment and freedom from fear and ignorance and any of the illusions that do keep you off the path and from your destination and your goal.

The Law of Facsimiles is the law that governs manifestation within the lower planes, for the physical emergence of the thing from higher realms is but a poor copy or facsimile of what was up above and the grandeur and the majesty of its reality in those planes from whence it was born and created. And so, to always remember, what you do want to create you must first imagine, and with the techniques of love and the secret initiatory word you can marshal of your powers and create the image and the face of the thing you most want to see in the world below, and by the Law of Facsimiles, with sufficient concentration and effort and diligence, it shall eventually come to pass and be seen and manifested here in the world below, as long as it does not contradict of any higher precedence and serves the good of all Souls concerned, to aid of best-laid plans.

The final law of good importance that I will be going to address is the Law of Consciousness. The Law of Consciousness does state that consciousness is the characteristic that defines the nature of Soul and what it is and how it relates to the reality in which it lives and has created. There is nothing beyond consciousness, nor anything less than it, as far as Soul is concerned, as a child in this universe and of the great Sugmad and from Its home in the Holy Spirit far above. And the unfoldment of the consciousness and its development and maturity is the process by which it grows and returns to whence it came and is able to become a contributing and powerful reflection of its Father far above. And so, the key thing to remember is always to look and see how does this relate to and affect one's consciousness abilities, and does it further one's progress on the path and one's own understanding of oneself and the secrets of the universe in which one exists and plays. And with this in mind shall you always find yourself well taken on the path and towards the heart of heaven, where every Soul does long to return and carry home.

Man, as Soul, is the walking embodiment of all truth. But how can this be? For certainly there can be seen many upon the Earth who do display and embody the highest levels of ignorance imaginable, and not a hint of truth or light may be seen, no matter how hard one looks. But this is not the case. Man, even in ignorance, is the embodiment of all truth. And this is how and the way that this is so. Truth is the fabric of existence, brought to the heart of man, as Soul, and awakened to return him to his home and to the heavens from which he originally came. Yet man, as he walks upon the Earth, does embody the truth that is the reality for his own stage and level of development and place upon the Earth. And so, if one does look broadly at all men in all places and levels and ways of unfoldment and development, then it can truly be seen the entire spectrum and embodiment of truth from all ages, cultures, and ways from which God is sought and found along the way and in each own distinctive and unique understanding and embrace. And also, one can look at man as the past, present and future all embodied in one but just living in the moment of experience at which he has found himself, depending on his level and abilities of understanding and knowledge of the ways and secrets of God. But when he opens his heart fully and listens to what it says, he does become the walking, living embodiment of all truth and love and wisdom that ever can be found and known within this universe of Sugmad.

The noble virtues that should be mastered and learned to aid the student in successful living are these. First, compassion, for this is the fastest, purest way to open of the heart and burn the heavy karma that has accumulated and piled so high upon the student's shoulders, to keep him from his home and departure from the Wheel of 84 and all the worlds below.

Second, diligence and focus, for these are the qualities that are most important to success along the path, and in the acquisition of the proper ways to act and the knowing of what is the best and surest way to quickly learn the lessons and progress along the path.

Third, discernment, for this is the key ability and virtue that does allow the student to, with skill and wisdom, truly see what is the proper way and decision in the difficult tests that come and are given to see if the student knows the way of proper action and is ready and prepared to advance upon the path.

And the final virtues are persistence and patience, for without these all is lost and all hope and inspiration and learning never shall take place unless the humility and gentle acceptance of the truth that must be won is pursued with these last virtues to speed the seeker on and bring him to the success that he does desire and deserve.

Unconditional love is a concept and practice much misunderstood in daily life and living. It does not mean to run about displaying

152

overt affections and bestowing marks of intimacy on all you do encounter, though this could be the case for those close within your immediate intimate circle. Rather it means to walk and act always in the neutral position and to carry and give detached goodwill and compassion to all, regardless of their station or offense against you, for if you will recall, all action requires participation from left or right to create enduring karma; and so, for those who wish to walk in service and a channel for the God-power, it is a critical thing to never respond with reaction from the left or to the right.

Now, this does not mean that one must become an emotional automaton, for this is not the case. One may still display and feel great depth and range of emotion and exuberance and warmth but from a remote and dispassionate place of detachment within the inner bodies. Though this sounds a tricky thing to do, it may be acquired with practice and study until at last the student does arrive at the place of perfect love and balance. And so, the final test and step in the equation is to give to all you meet the detached goodwill and compassion that is the perfected state and allows the God-power to flow through you from higher realms and enter into this physical world below.

To give unconditional love to all and practice this position and technique, the following exercise may be followed to facilitate the way. Upon rising each morning, and while bathing or contemplation, the student may repeat five HUs and then to the Master say "I wish to be a perfect vehicle for light for all I encounter today." And in this way shall the bodies be polarized to exemplify this state and give and show the love that is desired to be in the proper place.

The second way is, when you meet another Soul each day, to imagine the heart each time unfolding, like a rose in perfect bloom, and the light of God outpouring to reach the one you meet and stand with in friendship or whatever other circumstance. And in these ways will you become accustomed and truly begin to train your heart to be open and giving of the detached goodwill and compassion that is the key and way.

The atoms and molecules of the body are merely spinning orbs of light and electrical charge in different configurations to differently reflect and arrange the light of the eternal sun, and love is the power that moves and creates the universe and everything in existence. So, it is important to realize and know that the power of love, combined with strong projected feelings, can cause great change in the physical body at a subatomic and up to a molecular and physical level. This is to say that if the position of non-power is well achieved and maintained so that the God-power is flowing strongly and continuously throughout the physical shell, and if a feeling of love and warmth and caring always is held and projected to others and in the energetic bodies of one's self, this can lead to changes and greater vitality and youthfulness of appearance in the cells and features and organs of the one who carries grace. And also, it does then become possible to go within and seek the techniques and secrets to the physical body and aging that long have been the quest and bane of those who seek to slow the years and enjoy good physical health. So, keep always love in your heart and in your presence, and eventually you shall see the changes in your physical body that are a result of the grace and love that does flow through and within your heart.

The love between man and woman (or two who are together and close), though it does typically commence with the hormonal attraction of the lower chakras, with time and understanding can unfold and polarize into a manifestation of divine love here on Earth, for the power of love between two close-knit Souls does represent the perfect blending of the two great streams of energy and life in perfect balance and harmony and the expression of purpose and power within the physical realm, for perfect love is balance and magnitude of the flow of heavenly grace, and when a couple is in harmony and seeking only to give to the other, then their hearts are open and clear and the love of God can enter in and dance between the light and create a force and feeling of such power that nothing can resist its polarization and attraction of the love of others in their lives.

And so, when in relationship with one you love and care, the key to bringing your hearts to a place of openness and sharing is to always seek the opportunities to give love to the other, not necessarily with gifts or physical show, but with the feeling and unfolding of the heart, to let the love flow through and be felt and shared by the one to whom you share your heart and feelings. And over time and with practice as the fear does slip away and trust does grow and love does bloom, you shall awaken one day and feel the presence of divine love, such as you have never known, and this shall be the key and secret sign that finally you have succeeded and created here on Earth what was previously only known as a reality far in the heavens above.

"God helps he who helps himself." Though this has been said before and is a truth forever, it is well repeated and elaborated to further understanding and the application of the principle. Our thoughts are real things with force and presence and definition within the higher realms. And the feeling and position and direction of our thoughts, since they do emanate from such a high plane, determine the polarization of our lower bodies and the attraction or repulsion of what is drawn into or away from our life. And so, to make the greatest use of the divine power and creative force we should always strive to place our thoughts on the highest level possible, for in this way is our vibration and polarization raised and we are drawn close to the higher realms and the door is opened for the God-power to work with us and work through us, for when our thoughts are only focused on negativity and darker things, then these are what we do draw to ourselves. And so, for God to help us, we first must help ourselves, and it is by focusing on high thoughts and principles that this may be obtained and great success won.

To facilitate this connection, this simple technique may be used, though it does require some practice and determination, for each negative thought that comes within your head there is a positive complement that is the necessary existent other half of the equation, for no thought may exist without its dual unity of opposite proportion. And so, when you do find a negative thought slipping into your head and lodging itself there, consciously find its positive half and place it there instead as the object of your thought and fixation. And in this way shall you train the mental body to always seek the highest expression in anything it does, and

155

thus shall you begin to attract and draw the heavenly divine power into your life and to aid you in your cause and in your way.

The physical act of union between a man and woman is a sacred act and vehicle to connect with the light and truth of God. When two who do love one another connect in a physical way, this does serve to open of the heart and release the fears and anxieties that cloud the passageway and connection to Spirit and the flow of the God-power from above, for when in the tender embrace it is often easier to connect with and find the place of vulnerability and stillness and peace that is required to open the heart to the flow of the non-power of God. The key to success, while making love to your partner, for this principle does apply to those who find sweet repose and embrace with those of the same sex as well, is to go through the process and endeavors of getting to a place of trust and safety and vulnerability within the arms of the one you love and care for in your heart. However, this too is the challenge of this technique to open the heart to God, for too often is intimacy and sexual relations the place where things are brought that do represent the darkness and deepest fears and insecurities within the ones that play and are close to each other's arms and embrace. And so, what must be done is to declare the intimate act a sacred space of love and trust that never shall be violated or wrought apart as the sanctity of the loving sanctuary that is the heart exposed in the arms of the one you love. And when the two are able to finally find themselves in a place of utter trust and vulnerability, then both hearts can open and connect to one another and to the higher source, and this is when you shall begin to have incredible spiritual experiences while you do serve and play in the languorous arms of the one whom you do love so deeply.

The difficulty that the God-seeker can have in finding the right and compatible mate in life can stem from several reasons. First, the avid seeker on the path who is dedicated to his or her own course will accept no alternative nor brook any interference in his search and in his desires to find the gate of heaven and succeed upon the path. And if the person that is in his life does not share his fervor and enthusiasm or understand his commitment to the goal, then there ultimately will come a feeling of jealousy and resentment that there exists some other thing that exceeds in desirability the one

156

who is near and in the relationship of love, for it is most important, if success is to be found, that the two do share the love of the journey, and the difficulties and trials, and are committed to supporting one another as each does make his way amongst the lessons and trials that are brought to bear and be faced to teach each his own lessons and resolve of past life deeds and move forward on the path.

In addition, it can be a difficult thing, especially for the advanced seeker on the path, or those in The Way of Truth whose knowledge and understanding of the universe does far exceed most others, to truly find a one who will understand and know the same amount of what is known by the one who walks and prays and studies and does his contemplations daily to open the heart to God and unfold and develop to the birthright that is Soul and the glory to be won, for it is not an easy thing for either party to be romantically involved if one or the other is more educated and knowledgeable in the secret ways of God and of the universe and realms above, unless the one is willing to teach what he or she does know and the other is willing and desirous to learn and explore, as well, but this can truly be a difficult thing to find.

A third reason may be this: The Way of Truth Participant of high spiritual development and merit will simply have different goals and perspectives and desires from this life, for he can now see the limitations and futility of illusion. And so, it can truly be difficult for the one that he does draw near to understand his motivations or purposes in his daily acts and deeds. And this can lead to conflict and tension if the one who does not understand does find his ignorance threatening and seeks to make amends by asserting himself in different ways to compensate for this perceived inferiority or lack on his behalf, which does not truly exist, but is part of the illusion and the Kal that is always at play and at work to keep all Souls from God and the truth that they shall find in The Way of Truth and upon the great road home.

This problem does particularly apply to women, for men do have it easier because it is in women's nature to seek the teachings from the man, if she is in a trusting and loving relationship and does feel safe and free to be led to different ways of thinking and understanding of the heart and nature of God above. But men are more stubborn and insecure, and most are not willing to be with a woman who appears to know and understand more than he truly does. And so, it is more difficult for experienced women in The Way of Truth to find those few men who are either equal to them in merit and understanding or humble and willing to learn from one such as she who may have great wisdom to share, for many women who have come into a circle of achievement and merit that they themselves have earned to put off a vibration and frequency of confidence and power that the man who does not know himself, or has not explored of his own heart and its mysteries, does find intimidating and frightening, and this can be sensed and felt like the hare does sense the fox whenever its presence is near, for the ego and lower self of man is an assertive and powerful thing indeed, and in this way, he is disadvantaged in his development and his need for reassurance and safety to explore of anything that may require vulnerability and an exposure to possible pain and feeling deep in the heart. And for these reasons and others, will women in The Way of Truth truly find that some difficulty may be encountered to find a loving mate who is compatible and a good fit to their own self.

For the female participant in The Way of Truth who seeks to manifest a mate in a balanced and neutral way, the following technique may be utilized, although it must be understood that given the underlying dynamics already mentioned, and the role of human will, success may require great discipline and commitment to the path and the exercise that is given and shared. And even then, it may take some time to finally achieve the desires of your heart. To manifest the one you do desire, you may do the following technique.

When in quiet contemplation with the secret word or HU, gently see the Master standing in front of you or as the blue light of his love and protection and grace. Then, in the light, put yourself in a chair seated and facing him and next to you another empty chair shall you place and tell the Master humbly, with a heart full of love and hope, "Master, please fill this chair with the man who is spiritually compatible with me and who will serve the highest spiritual good of all concerned." And with repeated practice you shall finally find the one within your life who is a good fit and match to yourself and the goals of your two lives, and in this way may you enjoy a life of satisfaction and harmony in the arms of a beloved one who will join you on the path.

It is truly an important thing for the student to keep his sexuality balanced and sacred to prevent of anything that shall create any ripples or residual effect that may later come to haunt him on the path, for the physical sexual connection to another is the way that can be made as a gateway and a channel for energy to pass between the two, and not all that comes with another is known or may be benign. And so, to prevent the connection with dark energies and entities or other things unseen, it is important to keep the sexuality a sacred thing and space and act, that its intended purpose might be remembered and served to bring the student closer to the openness and love that is God's presence and loving light and truth that may be opened when the sacred space is remembered and created. Now, this is not to say that sex should only be reserved for marriage or done to procreate or prescribed by any other moral code that may be created and used by modern institutions to fulfill their will and ways and desires to have power over others of their flock. This is only to say that sex should be reserved and engaged in within a sacred space that reflects the sanctity and nature and divine manifestation that it does represent and can be used to achieve.

And so, to keep the sexuality sacred the following can be used and done, that the student shall be protected from any unseen harm and way. When the intimacy of the two does draw near, the student can, in his or her imagination, sing the sacred HU five times and imagine the two lovers surrounded by the blue light of the Living Sehaji Master and protected by his love and the truth and purity that he does represent and give. The second way is, if both lovers are participants in The Way of Truth, or open to the practice, to together sing the HU five times before the loving is begun, and declare together the presence of the Master to protect and watch over you and bring the sacred love and power of the Holy Spirit within the embrace you share. The third way that may be utilized is, before the night is begun, to sit alone in quiet contemplation and with a heart of love declare yourself a vehicle and channel for the

159

Sugmad, and that whatever does transpire between you and any other is the work of the Sugmad and you will faithfully proceed and, with a heart of trust, shall create a space of love and safety for the one with which you do find yourself near. And by using any or all of these techniques above shall the sanctity of the sexuality and its power be preserved and protected from unseen forces that may seek to do you harm or impede your progress on the path.

All true knowledge to be found is the Light and Sound of God. Though this may seem a difficult thing to understand or imagine, it is truly so, and this shall be explained. True knowledge is the wisdom and understanding of truth, of the secrets of the universe and Soul and how all does function and is governed within this realm of the Sugmad, beneath the cosmic Sea of Love and Mercy far above. And this truth and wisdom that comprises knowledge is given to man from above by sending it below, encoded in frequencies of Light and Sound that are sent by Soul and received by the heart and passed to the other faculties for decoding and integration and understanding by the lower bodies of man, for in the realms far above where Soul does reside and live, all knowledge is easily accessible to any who seek to look and understand what is the thing that does drive and cause of any other.

And so, as Soul does watch its lower bodies down below, it does retrieve from libraries and other Masters far above the truth and knowledge that is needed to be sent to its selves below to aid them on their way and in their understanding. And so, it must be seen and known and understood that all knowledge is Light and Sound, this is its form when it is stored and collected far above, and how it is sent to one below to aid him in his way and in his understanding.

True knowledge transcends space and time and has its foundation in the universal structure of existence itself. But how can this be? What does it mean? For this is no easy thing to understand or reconcile. So, we first shall begin with the first half of the assertion. True knowledge transcends space and time. And this we know to be true from our earlier discussion of universal eternal truth and its nature and fabrication as an extension of the very universe from which it comes, for eternal truth, which may also be characterized as true knowledge, does exist as immutable laws and

160

principles from the worlds of beingness above as have been given and discovered by the many mystics, saviors and sages that long have tread the worlds and studied in the heavens and the many realms above. For true knowledge is what is sought and given to those illumined beings who are worthy and have come and humbly beseeched of the Sugmad to share Its secret lore and the mysteries of Its universe and the functions of Its planes and the many things that do go on there and keep all cycles moving, with best-laid plans, toward the eternal goal. But, what then of the second half of our assertion?

True knowledge has its foundation in the universal structure of existence itself. The universal structure of existence is a matrix of Light and Sound that does combine and form in different frequencies and patterns, depending on the plane and world that is being formed, for these two elements are the building blocks and structure of all that ever has been created or destroyed, such is the nature of this universe of the Sugmad and all others. And so, as we do say, that the Light and Sound is the basic building block and structure of the existence of the universe, and we have already said and shown that true knowledge is Light and Sound, then it can be clearly seen, the linkage and connection that absolutely must be made, and does exist, between true knowledge, truth, and the universal foundation and structure of existence, for truth and knowledge are two very different things. One is an element, the other an aggregation, but true knowledge, the aggregation and organization of truth, is the building block and key to all creation and the basic foundation cell, which does comprise the construction of all the universes of God within creation of Its realms.

Relative truth and its conception is varied and understood differently from level to level, as has already been said previously in this chapter, yet eternal universal truth is unchanging within this universe. And so, it is to the student to learn to recognize and differentiate between the two in the course of his learning and unfoldment. As the student does ascend to higher realms, the relative truth does get closer in substance and content to absolute universal truth, and once the fifth plane of the lower dual worlds has been transcended, relative truth no longer does apply and then

161

all merit and further initiation is governed by the degree and depth of understanding of eternal truth and its subtleties and complexities and nuances that guide and hold the many hidden secrets of this universe of Sugmad. And so, as the student is struggling on the path within the lower worlds, he would do well to remember and always cast a critical eye on those things promulgated as truth, for it is the mark of achievement to be able to discern between the two, and between what is spoken and told in other paths and by other teachers, for this is a method of learning and lesson of achievement generally more applicable to those of other paths, for the teachings of The Way of Truth are the purest on the planet; and so, there is less need to dissect and ponder the teachings of our way. This lesson is more directed and given to aiding others on their paths and having compassion for what truths they may vehemently believe and hold close to their heart that is the way and lesson that they are mastering at that point in their journey on the path.

Truth is a postulation upon the mind of the human consciousness. It is the essential element of understanding brought from the higher planes that is recognized by the heart, but dissected and debated and rationalized and justified and finally accepted by the mind. And so, it can adequately and fairly be described as a postulation given to the mind by Soul for acceptance or denial, as is the test and purpose of that faculty in the progression and development of man. For if the mind does reject truth, then a situation of faith is created that must sustain until experience can overcome and provide the necessary evidence required by the mind, or until Soul can master the mental body and force its service and submission to the higher wisdom that is wielded and known by Soul, itself, as it does live and guide from beyond the Great Divide and is able to transcend the threats and temptations of illusion and negativity.

And for some, the eternal challenge in this life shall be to remain in a place of faith and inner knowingness, but without any justification or proof the mind can accept to believe in the postulations that have been put forth to it. And some may have many mystical and esoteric experiences that readily shall prove in an undeniable way the truth that is recognized in the heart. More shall be said of this in later chapters, but for now it is sufficient to say that truth is a postulation given to the mind, and then it is the

162

challenge and test as to how the mind shall react and deal with it in its own way and whose purpose it shall serve, those of its own, within the Mental Plane, or those of Soul, from beyond the Great Divide.

Man's greatest delusion is his belief that the causes of things that happen to him lie outside his own states of consciousness. But this is simply not the case. Everything that occurs in a man's life is a result of his own consciousness and awareness, even if he is not consciously aware of what is the true cause and purpose of the deed. Either he has allowed the situation to arise to repay a karmic debt, or he has created it to show himself some lesson he needs to learn, or he does relish the enjoyment as a pleasure of this life, but all things, and to this there is no exception, are created by his own hand within the inner planes or with his consent by others to achieve some other end or goal that is important to his unfoldment and lessons to be learned. And so, the purpose of the teachings of the path of The Way of Truth is to show man how to see behind the veil and understand the causes of what does come to him, and to use the hidden secrets of truth and the mysteries of God to efficiently manage of his payments and the lessons he must learn, and get to a place where he can begin to consciously create the life he desires that is free of karmic debt and in accordance with the service and harmony of Sugmad and Its best-laid plans for the unfoldment of all man and other beings within Its realms.

Tindor Saki (spoken directly and verbatim)

The goal of the student is to manifest truth moment-to-moment in this life, as experiences are had and seen, to move along the track and closer to the end of the life mission and contract, that the life that is desired can then be created and had, and to manifest truth in this sense means to always see beyond the illusion to the root cause and effect, and to know what esoteric spiritual principle of eternal truth does govern what is happening and how these truths can be applied to see the lesson learned and gain the wisdom and experience and successfully move on to quickly continue on the path. And this is done by maintaining the connection to the non-power and wisdom of the heart through the techniques already given in the chapters that have preceded this one. And so, the goal should be to maintain the detached and loving state and always seek the deeper truth and meaning that does come to you each day, and in this manner you shall gradually learn to be able to recognize the hidden dynamics and causes that lie unseen and how to resolve things quickly and move along the path.

The Holy Spirit was very persistent and clever to bring Its truth into my heart and life, when I was a student on the path, for I was not accustomed or well skilled in this art and ability, and I suffered many pains and troubles of illusion, as I did struggle to learn the skills and abilities to be able to discern what was truth and what was illusion in my daily life and living. But the great gift that Spirit does give in Its lessons and Its challenges is the countless opportunities that are had by the student to learn what must be known, for without these struggles and situations there would be no opportunity to grow and unfold and progress along the path. And so, the lesson to be learned, and for which I am eternally grateful to the Holy Spirit, is to view all challenges as opportunities and gifts from yourself and through the Holy Spirit to aid you in your path and in your learning to find the secret truth of God and ascend the top of the mountain where the greatest truth of all does await to bring you home to God.

Chapter Ten

The Heart of Heavenly Entrance

Leytor (spoken directly and verbatim)

Life upon the Earth and in the inner realms is a learning laboratory for Soul, so that it may prepare for the time and day when it will ascend to higher realms and assume its role and responsibilities in the higher worlds above. But like a child that must learn discipline and gain the experience of life and the consequences of the adult world, the Soul is sent below to, within the inner planes and Earth, learn the difficult lessons that often painfully must be learned. And the precocious Soul with the intuition of the heart well opened and received will quickly develop an intuitive grasp of the rules by which the game and experiment must be played, and with study and application, will advance quickly along the path. The young Soul, who is still blind to the rules of life and of the universe will clumsily bump about, and many errors make until, through a process of trial and error, it does begin to learn the ways and laws that govern this game of life. And so, within the laboratory, the entire spectrum does exist of developmental states of consciousness and awareness, from very high to very low. And it is the duty and responsibility of those who have made their way and ascended to the higher rungs to compassionately look back and aid of those who lag behind and are in need of patience and instruction to aid them on their way and in their difficulties. And so, this is the laboratory of life, through which all lessons are learned and all wisdom grasped, and this is its purpose and function, to educate of man as to the proper rules and ways of conduct within the higher realms above.

The happiness that each Soul seeks can never be found in outward things or other people but only deep within, for any love but that of God is only temporary and passing. And so, to find the eternal peace and deep happiness and contentment within the heart, it is a journey inward to overcome all things and find the love of God and the purpose of one's life and begin to work together with the mighty force of Spirit to become a conduit and vehicle to bring into other's lives the love that you have found and the end to fruitless searching and the never-ending quest for fulfillment and happiness within the illusion of the material realms, for any temporary happiness achieved through material acquisition or pursuit and victory is but a temporary thing and never can be completely satisfying at the place deep within the heart where truth is known and seen. So for all who seek the beauty and love of God and grace of Its power and wisdom to never leave their heart, do the exercises and techniques presented in the discourses and other places, and, with time, they shall achieve that love and peace and happiness they so desire within their heart and is their place.

Man and womankind's highest happiness is in their understanding of, and cooperation with, divine will and law, for the love and power of God is a force beyond imagination and not to be trifled with. And once the heart is opened to its mighty roaring flow, the greatest happiness and contentment may be truly found in understanding of its function and the secrets of its ways and cooperating and colluding with its desires for your life and your service to aid it in its cause. For the greater one is in alignment with the will of the Sugmad, the greater is the flow of God-power from the higher realms above, and the greater is the feeling of happiness and contentment at the work that one has done in alignment with the divine will and law. And so, to maximize the flow and power of the God-power through your heart and into the physical and other planes, seek wisdom and other words of grace and direction from the Masters in contemplation to aid you on your way and in your understanding of what is the proper way and direction of your actions to serve the will of the Sugmad, and enter the kingdom of heaven when you do come to go and leave forever this shell behind and the Wheel of 84, never to return again.

The seeker, as Soul, must strive unto itself for mastery of all the bodies, for this is truly the way that the riddle of life may be solved and the seeker shall escape the Wheel of 84 and continue on his way and into the heavens above, for each plane and its body is a riddle to be solved, and as the seeker gains in understanding and wisdom of the secrets and the rules that govern each plane, then self-mastery does begin, until the Soul has finally ascended all the dual planes below and has become a law unto itself of its reality and all that it does see and experience, for Self-Realization is the goal of the lower realms, and this does mean that the Soul no longer is perplexed by any riddle of any lower divided planes, and so does understand the mechanics and hidden secrets of the basic functions and ways that life may be conducted from a neutral and detached state so that all inner bodies do remain open and a conduit for the love and wisdom and truth of the higher planes above that Soul does send as instructions and teachings to its lower selves below. And once the self is mastered and the law is now understood and known, then the seeker can turn his attention to the higher realms above and deepen his understanding and broaden what he does know as he seeks the goal of God-Realization with the Ocean of Love and Mercy far above.

The quality of one's thought forms directly affect the God-seeker's survival here on Earth, for the thought forms of the seeker, when given persistent attention and emotional fuel, do descend within the bodies and finally do emerge as manifested reality in the Physical Plane on Earth. And so, it is imperative to train the mental body to always seek the highest in every thought it has, for this does directly affect the survival of the seeker here on Earth, especially when he does begin to ascend to higher realms and wield of greater power.

And the corollary to this thought is the notion that the thoughts, when properly managed and disciplined with love and structured to embody and support the highest principles of up above and the truth of the worlds of beingness, can bring a harmonious balance with the workings of Spirit down below and aid the seeker in finding and enjoying the life that he does desire to live while still in the service of the Holy Spirit and the Sugmad and Its wishes.

The moment-to-moment experience of life by the God-seeker is a never-ending parade of opportunities to tap the potentiality of its reality and enjoy the adventure of life. Love seeks others as a way to be expressed and felt and understood and received. And so, if the seeker does walk upon his day and daily activities with a heart full of love and joy, then each moment shall present the many potentialities to connect in some unsuspected way to another and fully enjoy and participate in the adventure of life, for the God-power is a dynamic, creative presence that always seeks to find a greater means and avenue of expression within the many Souls that do walk upon the Earth and other places and in each other's company. So do not let the fear of others' reactions or the rejection of their love or attention keep you from living well the adventure you are given to walk upon the Earth, and with an open heart to see and realize the potential that does exist within each moment to enjoy the adventures of life.

The words that we utter are part and parcel of the thought forms we have, but manifested in the Physical Plane and given root upon the Earth, and this is a powerful expression of the dynamics of manifestation, for words uttered from the lips do accelerate the cycles of descent and cause and creation that are the certain things that govern the rate and possibility of manifestation in the physical realm. For a thought form may exist within the mental body, but as soon as it is uttered, it has immediately descended from above and in one fell swoop and moment now has been connected and can live in the physical world. And especially for those who have great power, great care must truly be taken for the words that they do speak do open a vortex and a torrent of power that is grounded in the Physical Plane and accelerates the manifestation of the word and thought that was made. So, take great care in watching the thoughts and words that do come from you, for the Kal will take any opportunity to bring into physical life the manifestation of the negative power and energy. And as well, when only high thoughts and words are spoken, then the one wise upon the path does know and realize that he is creating pathways to heaven, for the opposite and reverse, as well, is true, that the pathways and lines of energy from high up in the Mental Plane can be traveled in reverse to further rise and gain in merit and the mastery of the lower Planes of God and the lower bodies of Soul.

And so, the words we impart to others are part of the heart of heavenly entrance, for the words we do create and share with others create linkages and pathways between other Souls. And if we are not careful to create these in a neutral and loving way, then these connections can weigh heavily and keep us tightly bound and within the lower worlds and hindered in our goal and journey of liberation and freedom. So, the safest thing to do is always, before the words are uttered, see them within your imagination and in your third eye as if typed across the screen of a computer, and in this way shall Soul have the opportunity to check and screen and modify for any leanings or charges to the left or to the right that could create unnecessary karma for the one who seeks to leave and journey onwards to other realms.

The purity of thought of the student is also part of connecting with the heart of heavenly entrance for the thought forms, as previously said, can create grooves and passages and pathways within the inner realms and up to the very gate of heaven at the top of the Great Divide that is the Soul Plane. And so, pure thought and high conceptions naturally gravitate to this region, for the fineness of their vibration does cause them to settle there, and this is a great step and advantage when the student seeks to elevate and place his consciousness as high as he can go to retrieve the wisdom and love and understanding of higher realms, for if the student, through a habit of pure thought, has established a resonance pattern high within the mental realm, then it is easier for Soul to reach down and there connect to it and gain for it the access of the heavenly gates above. And for this reason is it important to harbor thoughts of love and purity and high ideals to aid the seeker in his ways and undertakings.

A technique to facilitate a higher level of thought activity and purity is this: Throughout the day or during contemplation imagine of yourself upon the Mental Plane. And there imagine all your thoughts as balloons that are filled with air and floating all about you. Now, as you do wish to increase the activity and purity of your thoughts, imagine all the balloons as they begin to rise and are filled with golden light and sparkling diamonds that float within the air. And as these thought balloons do begin to fill and rise, they do collect in the highest possible region within the Mental Plane where it does meet the Etheric and Soul Planes. And as the final measure, imagine long cords of gold and silver attaching these balloons to your body on that plane. And in this way, with persistence and discipline and gentle training, shall the mental body learn and always focus its thoughts and activity on the purity of love and higher ideals in its workings through each day, and this shall aid the seeker and bring him closer to heaven's gates and his home above.

The living environment and relationships are a direct reflection of our spiritual environment, our travels, experiences and relationships in the inner worlds, for the Physical Plane is merely a shadowy, clouded reflection of the planes that exist above. And so, to gauge and see the state of our inner life, one can cast a discerning eye about and see what is present and transpiring within the world below in our daily reality and living. Of course, there can be a significant time delay in certain aspects and events, for not all reflections are manifested equally in relation to when they occur above. Some do happen at the same time, but some may take a month or a year or even more to finally make it to this plane. But the real value of looking at the physical reality and environment and relationships is as a useful gauge and measure of where you are and where you are headed. For example, in your relationships with other people, what are the types and kinds and characteristics that would describe the state of their unfoldment and spiritual awareness? What are the types of people that are entering into your reality? What are the types that are leaving? For this is a good method and barometer to gauge of your own progress and the direction of your travels.

The same may be said of your physical environment, not necessarily in terms of the value of things possessed, rather the organization and arrangement of physical objects within your life and living places. Are they neat and clean and organized and balanced in their proportion and aesthetic or are they messy and mixed and jumbled and cluttered with no coherent rhyme and function? For this too does say much about the coherence and discipline of the inner bodies and how they all do fit and function together. And so, the usefulness of this as a tool is to be used to ascertain the level and pace of your achievement and progress, and also where to further look and focus the efforts of your reaches, for with time and practice, you shall achieve the perfect balance and harmony in your outer world that is possessed and known within.

A powerful technique and method to bring harmony and coherence to both the inner and outer worlds is to relate to all life and living as if only you and Sugmad existed and all that did transpire in your reality was a conversation and dialogue between you and It, as to your learning and unfoldment and the refinement of your perception and inner abilities, for the goal in life perception is to see all in terms of balance and harmony and unity and wherever one does go to be the perfect expression of the love and God-power within the physical world. But to be this expression requires an eye and the ability to perceive at a refined level the fluctuations and tides of life. And so, to refine this perception and hone this keen ability, the God-seeker should, in his daily affairs and duties, always cast an eye about with the hope and the intention of seeking the manifestations of the Sugmad within every person and object that comes across his path. And with time and persistence, the seeker shall truly learn to see all with open eyes and perfect vision, for the truth it represents and the voice of Sugmad unspoken within the physical realm, in perfect balance and harmony with all that It does touch and affect.

God is one. Though this may sound a detached and esoteric concept with no practical application, this truly is not the case, for the God-seeker within himself can reach and discover the same oneness within him that connects him to all life and all creation. The explanation is not as complicated as it might first appear. Within the upper worlds of pure beingness and unity, all is part of itself and every other thing and consciousness. It is a shared consciousness and fabric of existence but interspersed with discrete units of conscious awareness that are the Souls floating in the sea. And all do know and can sense of all others and know their thoughts and feelings if they so choose. However, to do so would violate the free will and agency of the Soul, and this never would be done without explicit permission. But, nevertheless, the unity of connection and oneness still exists and underlies the nature of all existence within these higher realms.

171

Now, when the God-seeker does finally reach the detached and neutral state, then he is bringing the essence of this God-power within himself below and connecting to the oneness and unity of his true nature and true home far above in the heavens, above the Great Divide. And so, by this action and progression the God-seeker can truly find the unity and oneness that is God, and all Its Souls and universes within his own self and being. And this is what is truly meant by God is one, and the seeker can find this same oneness within his own self and being, as he progresses on the road and to certain greatness and glory.

Paulji once was known to say, "Man attains heaven, and heaven reaches the seeker when they are receptive to Its nature and open to Its influence." But what does he mean and how can this be accomplished? To say that man attains heaven and heaven reaches the seeker is rather an easier thing to understand, first. Man strives to open his heart and become a channel and conduit for the God-power of the heavens above. So in this way, he strives to attain heaven. However, the God-power needs to express Itself in lower realms; and so, It, as the Holy Spirit, does seek through Soul to enter the heart of the seeker and bring Its light and power and love to the lower planes. Thus heaven seeks to reach man on Earth. However, the key to understanding and success is to hear and be receptive to Its, to Sugmad's, nature and guidance and example and teachings, for by listening to Its heart and instructions and by emulating Its nature of perfect balance and detachment, by this way are the goals of both the seeker and the Holy Spirit brought to fruition and joined successfully as one. And so, this is what Paulji meant with this esoteric statement of such great wisdom and depth.

The experiences of the spiritual seeker on the path can be greatly varied in scope, breadth, intensity and frequency of occurrence. Some may have many experiences consciously out of the body, in vivid color, perception and remembrance. Others may have little besides the occasional occurrence of wisdom when his keen eye of discernment is well placed and paying attention. And all this does relate to the Life Contract and the needs of Soul as it develops and unfolds and, as well, to the toils of the Lords of Karma and the efficiency of the universe.

All Souls receive and are given in exact amount what is required to bring them in perfect balance with what they already know and believe and what they need to experience to take them to the next level and test of unfoldment and learning and initiation. And so, as well, the experiences the seeker has may vary at different times and places on the path, depending on how much progress was made in previous lives and how much is needed to be achieved in this one now, for it all is determined by what must truly be done by the Lords of Karma that the contract and learning is fulfilled, yet the Law of Economy is abided in all efforts they must do to keep the universe running efficiently and progressing toward the goal. To spend unnecessary effort to create for a seeker an experience that he does not need or require for his development is an out-of-balance action on the part of the Lords of Karma, and so must be balanced by somewhere else, removing from another seeker an experience he does need to aid him in his progress and next step on the path.

The exception to this is when the seeker beseeches of the Holy Spirit via the Master to, in a balanced way and method, bring to him a sign or experience related to his question or his query, for in this manner the desire of the seeker is blended via a specific request or desire with the creative power of the Holy Spirit, and in this way the experience may be created around the answer that is sought and thus the Law of Economy abided, and two birds killed with one stone.

And so, often it is the case, as well, that the life mission and contract of the seeker, and the duties and obligations and role that must be fulfilled, will require a certain amount of a certain type of experience to get the seeker to that place and enable him or her to do the duties he or she must do to fulfill his or her obligations and deeds. And so, in this case, the seeker might have many intense types of a single category of experience but none of another, for it is all governed and does relate to what the seeker has agreed to do in this lifetime.

And so, it is important to know and remember the role that faith does play in the other areas where the seeker might be lacking in certain types of experiences, for this is one of the tests of the path, to extrapolate the experiences had in one area or one manner to other places and areas based on faith and inner knowing and the wisdom and truth of the heart. And so, this may be a frustrating thing for many on the path; this is the truth of its occurrence and why it is done so that all does function in balance and harmony with all else that must be done and transpire in the realms below.

The seeker who is true to the nature of his thoughts and words empowers himself, as well as the life he is seeking to fulfill, because of the harmony and coherence that is generated by the alignment between thought and word and deed, for when one or two of the three are in misalignment, then the energy pathways are discontinuous and obstructed and there are greater delays in the effect and realization of the goals that are sought, for it serves no advantage or benefit to say the proper things and act them in daily life, if the thoughts and heart do not share their same nature. The gates of heaven cannot be bought with false words or actions down below. They must be gained with truth of thought and feeling and intention, for this is truly the way that the torrents of love and truth are opened and the power of God is brought down into the realms below. And so, the seeker who maintains thoughts and words of a lofty and pure nature, and does accompany these with similar intentions and deeds, does find himself well and quickly advanced along the path and much sooner at the gates of heaven than otherwise would have occurred were the coherence and alignment not achieved.

Each seeker is an autonomous Soul and free and independent in its own right, and it is a lesson and the duty and a test of each Soul to respect and have compassion for the right to choice of self-direction by each other Soul upon the path, for this is the thing called spiritual freedom and it does truly mean the right of every Soul upon the path, whichever it may be, to choose the method and pace and reality that is the desired way for it to have the experiences to which it has agreed. And so, it is to you the challenge to give to those you love the right and freedom to have the experiences that each alone must face no matter how difficult or painful it may be to see the other struggle with some lesson or difficulty that you have already mastered and learned, for you must not interfere in the lessons and tests of another unless the one you love has specifically requested and given permission for you to interfere and aid as you see fit. And then, the test and lesson, of which you must be aware, is of how to give love and guidance without taking on the test and burden of the difficulty that is created to be borne by the one to whom it has been manifested.

A single-minded focus on Self-Realization and God-Realization by the seeker does bring upliftment and love and breaks some of the chains of karma of those who are held near, for when the seeker does remain intensely focused on the goal and disciplined in his practice, then he does begin to channel greater amounts of wisdom, light, and love, and all those to whom he is connected by bonds between the hearts do, as well, receive of the benefit of his single minded focus and efforts to make the journey home. And the searing power and love of God that he does bring to Earth does uplift and burns away certain of the karma that is borne by those whom he loves and does hold near. And this is a service and means by which he does express his love and, as well, accelerates the resolution of his own karma by the deeds of love he does in service to others and the Holy Spirit.

You are the present sum of all your pasts and all your potential futures, and by your learning and ability to transcend time and space and draw upon your own creative and God-powers, you do have the endless opportunity and ability to create the life you want and fulfill your personal desires and goals, for even within your life mission and contract there is infinite variability and options in the way in which the terms and conditions may be fulfilled, and you do have all of your past lifetimes and experience that can be used to create the perfect life you desire in your present physical shell and incarnation. And so, one should not become frustrated by the perceived limitations and restrictions of the physical reality that is known, for it is within the grasp and abilities, as each does get closer to its home, to consciously create the life that is desired with the abilities that are had and the endless possibilities that are possible, when you do only know how to utilize the powers you do have, and shall come to understand, as you do progress upon the path.

175

The guidance of the heart is truly the thing that places the God-seeker on the razor's edge of life, compared to the guidance of the mind, for the guidance of the mind does only take the God-seeker deeper into the illusions, if it is allowed to go unchecked. The guidance of the heart must be used to balance the mind in all matters and keep to the neutral path, for upon this fine point of neutrality is the positive equaled by the dark, and in its perfect center may the heart fully open and speak the wisdom of higher realms. So, the goal and aspiration of the seeker should be to keep the negative and positive powers of the mind balanced, and in that center place of being neither for nor against, shall the magic and true light and guidance of the heart be found.

The Key to the Heart of Heavenly Entrance

"The seeker walks the Earth alone,
But never should he be feeling,
Without the hand of Sugmad's arm,
Upon his heart with healing.
The long arm of the One above,
Does reach here far below.
And gives the guidance and the love,
To all who bend in kneeling.
The heart of heavenly entrance known,
To all true sages and Masters,
It is the task of pain to learn,
The manners of the healing,
And opening of the heart.
The open heart with love a flow,
Does truly guide the seeker.
And he who gives his self to walk,
The path that he is shown,
Shall quickly find that he is led,
Along the twisted stones,
And to the heart of heaven.
So remember this, my seeker friend,
To always trust the feelings.
And guidance that comes from above,
And through the heart of healing.
For this is the key to journey home,
And none other is there truly,
That opens up the gates above,
And grants you Sugmad's healing."

This shall be the poem for all seekers of heaven's gates with open hearts of love.

(End of Lai Tsi's dialogue)

The heart of heavenly entrance is an important thing to know for the techniques and principles given herein. Though many do sound simple and not as deeply esoteric or confusing as others that have been given, do not confuse complexity and difficulty of understanding and practice with the inherent power of simplicity, for often those things that will move us farthest along the path are truly the simplest. And so, I urge all seekers to carefully study and ponder what has been here said, for much great wisdom and guidance does lie within these pages of the secrets of love and the heart and the entrance to heaven's gates. Open your heart to love and truth, and the heavens shall reach out and find you, as they are guided by the Master's hand. This is the promise and the truth to those upon the path of The Way of Truth.

Chapter Eleven

The Key to All Realms

Leytor (spoken directly and verbatim)

Student of the teachings, I do share with you the great true wisdom to aid you in your journeys. Love is the heart of all that does exist and all that is pure and worthy of receiving. Human love is not that thing that opens the heavens to you; it is the love of God and Its pure truth that shall lead you to certain glory. Walk always with your heart open to the love of God's great wisdom and power, for those who are able to truly surrender to Its ways shall find the entire kingdom of heaven lain open at their feet. Walk always with one eye towards the heavens, and one ear turned to listen for the subtle whispers of God leading you onward to glory and greatness. The love of God does steal upon you like a whisper in the night on the soft breath of a fresh blossom's breeze. Listen truly for its call to lead you back to the warm embrace of Its encompassing and forgiving heart. The man who does walk always with his heart open to the love of God is the man who does soon hear the heavenly choir singing softly of his gentle praises in the quiet of his heart. Do not forget that love is truly the key to all matters, and truly the heart of all success, for there is no other way.

The initiations you do receive are keys to opening the doors to higher Planes of God. You will find yourself with a home in a new world of God, with greater power, wisdom, love and awareness. As you do become accustomed to the flow of your new powers, the heart of God shall begin to flow through you more strongly and energize and uplift of all your inner bodies. All parts of your life shall find a greater clarity and understanding, and you now will wield of greater power to obtain of all that you do seek. You shall gradually grow in proficiency, as you do learn the rules and means of operating within this new state of being, and the lessons you do well learn shall guide you ever onwards on the never-ending journey back to God.

With the new initiation, you have ascended another rung on the ladder back to God's heart. The starry skies do ever stretch before you, yet your accomplishment does bring you the rewards of greater love, power, and wisdom. Do not rush to flee from your new home and seek of higher realms, for all of eternity does wait for you to learn of all God's lessons. You have taken another great step to return home to God's arms, and It is happy at your striving and success along the path. Be ever vigilant with your deeds and actions and continue in your toils, for soon It shall welcome you finally, into Its heavenly home.

The gift of the initiation does bring with it great responsibility to all of life and all Souls. You will wield of a greater power and have a greater understanding, and the gift is not given without the expectation of greater service, for you will have the responsibility to guide and teach of all who seek and strive for the wisdom you have achieved. It is God's great plan and purpose that none shall receive of the gifts of grace that do not use them to enrich the lives of others. Enjoy the fruits of your success and merit, yet do not linger on your laurels, for you must continue with the plan and aid of other Souls. These gifts are freely given from the heart and love of God, yet the student who does apply them shall forever gain in merit and ascend to greater heights.

The terms "awareness" and "Soul-awareness" do relate to and mean the ability to hear and know and understand the wisdom and truth and love that is given by Soul to the lower bodies to aid it in its cause and ways. It is the ability to quiet the mind and lower self and hear and know and feel the awareness and wisdom of Soul, for when the student is in contemplation, or at other times when the higher wisdom does come through, these are examples of Soul-awareness and the truth that it does give. Now "awareness," as a term unto itself, does merely refer to the consciousness of our reality and what does occur and progress there. And each body on each plane does have its own truth and level of awareness that is to be mastered and understood and controlled to succeed to higher realms. And the lower self, or ego, is the composite of all the awarenesses of the lower bodies, as they do combine and meld together to create the lower self of man. And it is the awareness of these bodies that must be mastered and aligned and kept in the neutral, detached state to allow the Soul-awareness to shine through and speak the truth of higher realms.

Soul-awareness and Self-Realization are bound and interrelated. Soul-awareness is the conscious ability to hear and perceive through the faculty of the Soul body. Self-Realization is the knowledge and connection to the true self, Soul. And Soul-awareness is achieved by mastering the lower bodies of the lower self. And so, for one to be Self-Realized means that he has mastered the ego or lower self and now is conscious of, and connected to, the higher self, Soul; and so, this is how these two do interrelate.

Awareness in the Physical Plane is vastly different from that on the Astral, Causal, Mental or Etheric, for within these inner realms, Soul is not so bound by the limitations and distractions of the physical world, for these are all much more fluid and liquid environments and more malleable and responsive to the powers of thought and intention. And so, within the physical realm, awareness is generally focused on immediate present events and circumstances, and it is the task of the seeker to learn to hear and feel and recognize and master the different awarenesses of the different bodies amidst the cacophony and noise and distractions of the physical reality here; whereas within the inner realms all is more quiet and stable and coherent, and it is a simpler thing to perceive and understand the different functions and abilities of the different bodies and how they may be used.

Within the inner planes, the reaction time between cause and effect is much shortened, and, so, this does greatly accelerate the process of learning and mastery of the different bodies and their abilities. Because the physical realm is so dense and coarse in vibration, it is much more difficult to see the correlations between cause and effect; and so, the awareness must have a much higher level of discernment to achieve the same progress and goals. And this is the reason that mastery of the lower self, or Self-Realization, must be achieved within the physical realm before the Soul can be released from the Wheel of 84, for if it is able to master itself in the most challenging environment, then it shall be able to manage and succeed of anything it should encounter above.

The awareness in the physical world and planes does vastly differ from the awareness in the worlds of beingness above the Great Divide that does fall between the etheric and Soul Planes. In the physical world, the awareness is limited in scope, function and ability because of the denseness and coarseness of this plane, which does limit the ability of perception to short distances and times and spaces, as it does pertain to the perceived immediate reality of the seeker's own place and time. However, within the worlds of beingness, the vibrations are much finer and transparent; and so, the awareness can penetrate much farther and the perceived reality of Soul, of the creative unit of awareness, does stretch infinitely farther than it does in realm below. It is the difference between peering through a glass and into foggy weather, or from the mountain top, so vastly different is the vibration and ability to perceive and know all that does exist. Within the physical world, the awareness is necessarily limited, so the disciplines can be developed, for there is a minimum of damage that Soul can do within the lower planes when its scope of influence and perception is held to the narrow confines of its own reality and understanding. But in the worlds of beingness, the Soul is more disciplined, and so has access to greater power and the fuller use of its abilities and perceptions. And so, it is a vast difference between what is known and done and experienced within planes above and those below, as Soul does learn and grow and progress upon the path.

The elements of time and space have a compounding effect on the limited perceptions within the Physical Plane, for time does bring the perception of reality in discrete units of space and experience, and this is food for the mind to limit and confound its ability to perceive beyond these limits, as is done in planes above the Great Divide, for time and space are the framework and foundation upon which the illusion of the dual worlds is built. The mind uses the perception of time and space to categorize and place events and circumstances, and in this way does create a system of logic and conclusions that is the cage to keep man from realizing his higher self and truth. Time and space do not exist within the worlds of beingness, for there is only now, and now is wherever the attention is placed along the spectrum of experience and the continuum of the chosen path. And, as well, there is no space, for now is here. And where the attention is placed is where Soul is, and in this manner there is no perception of time passing, while distance in space is traversed, unless it is desired, so as a whimsy and artifact of a Soul with humorous taste, for to place the attention in a situation or idea is to instantly be there without the passage of time or perception of travel. And so, all this is to say that time and space are elements of existence within the Physical Plane that are devised and used by mind to create the labyrinth of illusion that so effectively bonds man here and limits his awareness to what is immediately near his face and senses, until the Soul is awakened to the truth and experience of higher planes.

The elements of time and space, as well, affect the way that manifestation is brought into being. Because of the density and slowness and coarseness of vibration within the Physical Plane, it takes much longer for the manifestation of objects and situations from within the inner planes to descend, because of the friction of not only the molecules of matter and life, but also the interference of vibrations from the free wills and untamed and undisciplined inner bodies of all who walk on Earth, for the physical realm is not a pure and coherent state, as are the worlds of beingness above where creation and manifestation is done instantly in a balanced and neutral way. In worlds below, the confounding elements of time and space do, as well, limit the expectations and understanding of what is possible to be achieved and undertaken to manifest what is done above, for it is not a singular act, but one that requires participation from others who are involved, and because of the reality distortions of individual perceptions of time and space, it is very difficult to gain a coherence of action and intention among the many Souls that are required to manifest things in the Physical Plane. And, as well, this is why it is easier for manifestation to occur within well-trained teams of individuals who have worked and disciplined themselves and do share a tightly coherent consensual reality of what is possible and how it may be achieved. And so, these are some of the reasons that manifestation is much slower to achieve within the physical world of man.

Physical and Soul-awareness can be used in conjunction to improve the quality of life. When the physical reality and awareness is utilized in a balanced state, then the wisdom of Soul-awareness can be heard and received to guide the better life of man. And, conversely, the Soul-awareness does need the direct perceptions and feedback to gain an accurate understanding of what is transpiring in the physical state, for it must be recalled that the perspective and vision of Soul is from a much higher place, and it is not always accurate in its understanding of the circumstances and events that do happen down below. And so, it is a complimentary relationship that must be developed to maximize the skills of each: the physical-awareness providing accurate data of the circumstances below, the Soul-awareness rendering advice and guidance from its perspective and access in higher realms, and the physical–awareness, again, enacting faithfully the instructions of what the higher self does give to guide it successfully on its way to a better life and greater understanding.

As the seeker does progress positively along the path, a balanced inflow and outflow of spiritual energy is required, for if too much spiritual energy is released without being replenished by sufficient inflow, the seeker shall be left exhausted and in a deficit and shall not have the energy to continue or move within the inner realms, for this is an out-of-balance position that leaves the one too weak to successfully carry on. As well, a seeker who has too much inflow and insufficient outflow does become bottled up and spiritual indigestion does occur and the seeker is then shut down from further addition until the energy has had a chance to dissipate and regain its balance. And so, the key to successfully moving forward on the path is to try and find the balance and equilibrium between the love and power and wisdom that is shared and given and that which is received, for in this balanced position is the seeker gradually moved higher on the ladder, and the volume that can pass through the inner bodies slowly does expand, as the seeker does gain in merit and power and initiations.

Surrender is the final step and key to Self-Realization in this lifetime. Surrender means complete trust and co-workership with the Holy Spirit to guide of all your daily affairs and living, even when the mind does try to interfere and lead the one astray, for if the seeker does maintain balance and has learned to hear the voice of its higher self, and if the spiritual tools are known and used in their proper way, then all of the seeker's life and energy and purpose is blended with the Holy Spirit and he is directed and protected and shown the surest way to find and achieve the life he does desire. However, the problems arise when the mind does assert itself and tells the lower bodies the advice and guidance of Sugmad makes no sense and to go the other way. However, how can the mind have the wisdom or perspective of the Holy Spirit, which is the voice and will of Sugmad Itself? It cannot. And for this reason, the key to Self-Realization is the surrender that must be achieved by the student to finally win the battle and achieve the prize that has been sought, for without surrender to the guidance of the Holy Spirit and the higher self, the way can never be won.

Self-recognition and self-responsibility are two important steps on the way to Self-Realization. Self-recognition does relate to the ability to see and understand and master each of the inner bodies that do comprise the lower self or ego. Self-responsibility does mean that the seeker accepts and takes full responsibility for the actions and consequences of what is done by his inner bodies and their deeds, for Self-Realization is the mastery and control of the lower inner bodies to become the law unto yourself, and without the important steps of self-recognition and self-responsibility, this state and goal can never be attained or achieved.

The statement, "Soul is a historical document," is an important thing to understand, for it does hold the key to much wisdom and power. Soul has memory of all the actions of all the lifetimes it ever has lived on Earth or any other place or planet; and as Soul, matures and becomes more skilled in its own faculties and abilities, this memory does become an endless source of understanding and wisdom to aid it in its current situations and difficulties, for the patterns and Souls and trials that are faced and experienced each day along the road to Self-Realization do mostly have a basis and root cause in some action from the past. And so,

185

to be able to recall and understand the nature of the situation from the many lifetimes ago can speed the resolution or prevention altogether, for it all does depend on the skill and ability of the student. As well, as one does mature and draw closer to and begin his life mission, the skills and abilities that were known in other times or from between lifetimes can be remembered and reawakened to aid the student on the path and in his duties. And so, it can be seen and known that the Soul is a historical record of unbelievable proportions and benefit when it is properly understood and utilized.

After the God-seeker attains Self-Realization, the human mind and will still have a productive role to play. The mind is now a tool to be utilized by Soul to complete of computational tasks similar to what a computer could be programmed for and used to do. However, now it is guided and directed in its efforts and its focus by the voice and wisdom of Soul. Similarly, the mind and will can be applied to situations and conditions to find the strength and focus to serve the desires and purposes that Soul does put it to. And so, the key understanding and condition that must be known and seen is that, in the former state, the mind and human will make and enforce the decisions and only served themselves, and in the latter of Self-Realization, the two are put in service to the desires of the higher self and the doing of its wishes. And in this way, the mind and human will find their appropriate roles, and serve the function for which they were designed and originally created.

The majority of the students are unable to unlock and assess and utilize the keys and abilities and powers of their initiations effectively. Though it does differ from Soul to Soul and by their level of initiation, in general, blockages in the root chakra and a lack of imagination and valor and curiosity do limit the abilities of the students to maximize what they are able to do, for the blocked root chakra does prevent the student from grounding the power of their circle within the physical realm. And this does lead to a decreased ability to wield the power of the circle and do what should be able to be done. Of the other, it speaks to the timidity and lack of imagination on the student's part, which is an artifact of the last age when Souls were told what to believe and do and did not venture spiritually for themselves or seek their own truth and the limits of their abilities.

And so, the students of today do need to be more creative and aggressive in inventing their own ways to use the power of the Holy Spirit and of their circle to do what can be done to overcome the trials of life upon the path, for a technique does not have to be given by a Master to be effective and achieve the desired end. The spiritual laws and principles are given to all Participants in The Way of Truth to give them the tools and knowledge that they might venture out and use their own creativity and inspiration to create what they do need to aid them on the path and in their struggles.

Of assistance, as well is the following technique that may be used to open the root chakra and ground the flow of energy to this Physical Plane below.

Agnotti (spoken directly and verbatim)

Always there are opportunities to make progress towards the goal. Clearing the root chakra is merely one stop on the path back to God. There are many others. Begin by imagining yourself to be a column of light. Then move slowly down until you reach the lowest level, the root chakra. Begin to see a gently pulsing wave of energy slowly moving up the column of light and back down again. This up-and-down rhythmical wave motion gently dislodges and dissolves blockages and opens the chakras to greater flows of Light and Sound. End by withdrawing the column upward, slowly leaving a clear open expression of space at each level. Repeat this exercise several times over the course of a few weeks.

Kadmon (spoken directly and verbatim)

At times, there will be the need for this exercise. Many have great difficulty allowing the God-energy to pass freely through them. This wisdom is thus very important to man. To clear this chakra, do as Agnotti has instructed. It also helps, though, to chant or repeat the secret word or HU as the exercise is undertaken. This brings added strength to the process and more efficiently removes blockages and dross. Do this several times over the course of a few weeks or until a lightness is felt.

(End of Kadmon's dialogue.)

Leytor (spoken directly and verbatim)

The other technique that is recommended to gain access and understanding of the abilities and scope of power of the initiation is to do the following. In quiet contemplation, see the Master's face and blue light, and then to say to him humbly, "Master, when I am faced with difficult situations, when I would benefit from insight and the power of my initiation, please show these things to me." And in this way, when the student is faced with some difficult situation or task or problem, then the Master shall aid in opening his heart and eyes to the solution that is available, to do what can be done and fully maximize the power of the circle and initiation.

In some instances and occasions, the student's initiatory word can seem to run out of power and cease to function. This can occur for several reasons, however, the most common of which is that the mind has become aware of its usage and has moved to block its reach, and so retain of its own power and dominion. When this does truly occur and is experienced, several options do exist for the student. The first is to go in contemplation and tell the Master of the situation and ask for his assistance to restore the power of the word. The second is to go again in contemplation and ask that a new word be given, and then, if it is not immediately received, to watch the ebb and flow of daily living for the answer which will come.

The Life Contract of the student may change after Self-Realization is attained, for the specifics and conditions contained within the contract up to that point do pertain to and relate to the instances and lessons and trials that are required to bring the student along the path and finally to the goal. However, it is the responsibility of the student as to how far and how fast along the path he does wish to travel, and for those who wish to avoid pain and suffering and the trials of difficult lessons, they may meander along the path and only with reticence and distaste proceed from one lesson to another. Whereas, the God-seeker who wishes only to complete his task and attain the goal of his perception will fearlessly face and master every difficult lesson that is placed before his path. And so, in this matter are the terms and conditions of the Life Contract, as it does relate to achieving Self-Realization fulfilled.

Once the goal is attained, however, the seeker's obligations have been fulfilled and now the next leg of his journey may commence, and this is a wholly different matter as to the experiences and occurrences that now do come into the Self-Realized seeker's life, for now the great challenges and lessons have passed, and the student is now set to fulfill his purpose and mission as a co-worker with Sugmad. In the Life Contract, this second section is delineated as to what is the way and course that this service may be fulfilled, but as the Soul has grown in strength and wisdom and understanding and mastered the lower selves, there is now the opportunity for negotiation and rewriting of what the obligations and terms and conditions of service truly are. And it is at this place that the student can begin to shape the life he does desire to have and live within this plane, for there are many ways to blend the will of human desire with the power and wisdom of the Holy Spirit, and so obtain all physical conditions that are sought, but, as well, serve the highest spiritual interests of all who are involved and are affected by the one who has reached the level of Self-Realization and undertaken the task.

To begin the process of rewriting the Life Contract after Self-Realization has been reached is a simple matter indeed. It does entail going to Shamus i Tabriz, the Living Sehaji Master, and the Lords of Karma and seeing what does lie ahead for the seeker in his remaining days, and then, evaluating his position and how it does relate to the things he does desire to have within his life, as he does continue on his way. Then, suggestions are presented by the seeker to Shamus and the Living Sehaji Master and finally to the Lords of Karma until all do finally agree on a set of terms and conditions that do fulfill the needs of Sugmad, and, as well, do bring to the student the life he truly seeks. And in this way is the seeker's will blended with the Spirit and the life mission and contract is amended to serve the needs of all.

Certain elements of the student's experience, however, may not be rewritten or changed, such as some physical illness or mental maladies. For these are major terms of agreement between the Soul and the Sugmad, as created and constructed by the Lords of Karma, to keep the minimum balance needed within the worlds of Its domains. For it is like the terms of a written contract in that some are more inflexible than others, and while some may be renegotiated by any with the merit and experience and understanding to do what must be done, some are essential to the Soul's payment and unfoldment of all earned karmic debts, and so may not be shifted but merely must be endured until the debt is paid and the student may continue on. However, whenever the student does question if this is the circumstance and case, he should go to Shamus i Tabriz or to the Lords of Karma to inquire if it is something that is negotiable or if it must be weathered like the fury of the storm that cannot be delayed. The one exception is this, and that is if the student does wish to permanently delay the goal of Self-Realization until another lifetime has passed, the ailment may be delayed until the next incarnation. However, it must be understood that due to the delay and the work that is required by the Lords of Karma to rebalance of all debts and other conditions, the payment may be increased to compensate for what must be done and the grace that was given in this life to delay the debt to be faced.

Those who possess the power of the Self-Realized state will have others drawn to them who seek their emotional, mental and physical energy as the unsuspecting moth is hypnotized and drawn to the flame. And so, the Self-Realized seeker must learn to use the power and skills of his initiation to discern and truly see what the intention of those about him is and what the deep desires that burn within their hearts are.

To discern the true intentions of those within your sphere, the following techniques may be used. First, go in contemplation and within the Master's light see the face of the one in question and ask of him the truth of his intention and why he does come to you. The second is, as well, in contemplation to speak to the one itself or its Oversoul and ask again the question of what is it that he does seek by coming into your reality and presence. The third way that may

190

be utilized is, when you are in the presence of the one, imagine you both within the light of the Master and silently sing three HUs and you shall receive a sign or intuition of what are the true desires and intentions of the one who comes to you. Each of these techniques is equally powerful and valid. It is simply to the choice of the Self-Realized one to which he does prefer and wishes to use to aid him in his way and his endeavors.

Kadmon (spoken directly and verbatim)

For those seekers on the path who have achieved Self-Realization and God-Realization, the hearts of men bear few surprises. Though this can be a disheartening thing to see, it is truly so, for men in their ignorance and error upon the path do frequently betray the words that pass their lips and the intentions and high ideals that they do often speak of and endorse. And so, for the Self-Realized and God-Realized, the vision of the heart and higher self is perfect, and regardless of what men say, their truth and hearts and intentions are clearly known and seen, for one of the tests of the God-Realized is not the ability to know all about a man, as he does peer within the heart, it is to always abide the Law of Silence as to what has there been seen and understood as to the truth of that Soul and its position and intentions and development on the path.

To be in this world in a balanced way, yet not of it, is the challenge and goal of every seeker on the path, for what this means is that you do walk within the physical world of man, but you are not buffeted and tossed about by the winds of illusion and change. You are steadfast and immovable, as the stone in your neutrality and detachment, to stay the one true course and upon the wisdom and understanding of the heart and higher self, for though you do walk in physical realms, your consciousness and guidance does remain rooted and connected and brought from higher realms beyond the planes of illusion and duality. And so, this is what is meant to walk within the world of physical reality but not be of its illusion and negativity and veils.

To stay balanced in this world, however, does require certain vigilance and discipline to maintain the connection to the higher self and inner planes and yet still function well as a contributing member of society and to your fellow man. And the technique that may be utilized to have all balance kept is to be steadfast in the practice of the spiritual techniques and exercises that are given in this book of wisdom and other discourses and to always cast a discerning eye upon each situation to learn to see and walk and practice the razor's edge of perfect balance while within the physical realm.

When the grace of Sugmad was finally reached and Self-Realization was attained, after many years of toil and struggles upon the path, there were immediate gems of wisdom that were quickly given to me that did ease the burden of my suffering and long journey on the path, the first of which was the understanding that the goal could be obtained and was not so far away, as I had believed and imagined. Indeed, the shift in consciousness and awareness was less profound and difficult than I had at first imagined, and this gave me great inspiration and renewed dedication to continue in my ways and in my toils to serve of the Sugmad and aid of other Souls who struggled on the path.

Second was the vision and understanding of the magnificence that is I, Soul, my true higher self and being, and of the power I possess once I am able to realize it and wield it in a way that is responsible and disciplined and serves the will of Sugmad and the highest interests of all. And, finally, was the realization and understanding of the perfection and balance of all that is and the harmony that does exist, even within the horrors of man and his deeds of ignorance within the lower planes, for I could now more clearly see the myriad kaleidoscope of cause and effect that drives of all the cycles of action within all the realms of existence within this universe of the Sugmad. And so, these are a few of the gems of wisdom that fell upon my feet when I was able to obtain the Self-Realized state of initiation.

The vigilance and discipline required to achieve the Self-Realized and God-Realized states is complete and sometimes difficult to imagine and attain. However, perfect vigilance, control and discipline does extend to every body of the seeker within the inner planes, and every thought and action of his life, to include his thoughts and feelings, for in the Self-Realized and God-Realized states you cannot exist as effect, you must become the neutral personification of the state of cause and effect in one and in the balanced and perfect manner of expression, and if perfect control and discipline has not been mastered, then this state may not be obtained and held. And so, I give this poem to inspire those upon the path to continue in their struggles and the toils they do face to achieve the final goal.

Poem for Struggling Seekers

"When the heart is open,
And the love is pouring in.
Then the seeker knows that,
He has attained the place.
Of perfect wisdom, truth and understanding,
That shall guide him in his ways,
And to the final goal.
Yet along the way and journey,
Many are the tests to be faced.
And it is to the seeker,
To continue in his ways,
And not abandon the heart of truth and wisdom.
For the challenge is the discipline,
And control that must be sought.
To master the illusions,
And the winds they do create.
To take the seeker far afield,
Of the goal that he does seek.
And the truth and loving comfort,
Of the heart of Heaven's gates.
And so, the key is vigilance,
Of the bodies and their state.
And perfect control and balance,
Of all that they do say and do,
To keep you from your goal.
For discipline and knowledge,
Truly is the key.
And if the seeker continues,
And always casts about.
The eye of discerning observance,
He eventually shall see.
And be able to follow,
The center path before his feet,
And succeed in his endeavors."

And this shall be the poem to inspire all vigilant seekers on the path. The path of Self-Realization and God-Realization is a universal process that transcends space, time, species, planets and universes. All Souls, in whatever form or society or age in which

194

they do exist, do follow the same pathways and trials as they progress along the path, for this is the structure and function and purpose of the universes of God. And so, within the reincarnative process, many Souls are reborn and do live and, for a time, exist on other planets and in other bodies of other species and forms of life. However, Souls are often veiled from the memory of these lifetimes that were had on other planets, for the memory of interplanetary reincarnation would be too great a shock to many who are newly on the path or not so advanced in their understanding. But as the student does progress, if he does wish to know and remember of other lifetimes on distant planets past, he may go to Shamus i Tabriz and humbly ask to be shown the records and memories of the lifetimes he has had on other planets and as other species and forms of life. And in this way shall he come to understand the purpose and unity and oneness of all life and purpose within the universes of God and all seekers on the path, regardless of their face or body or language.

Paulji (spoken directly and verbatim)

The truth has at times been spoken and said that "assertions about the Word are assertions about ourselves." But what does this esoteric statement really say, and how can it be applied to our daily life and living? The Word is the Holy Spirit or the voice and will of Sugmad. It is how It enacts and communicates and fulfills Its wishes and desires within all Its universe and many planes and planets. But how does this relate to us? When an assertion is made about the Word, that assertion seeks to make some statement from the perspective and awareness of the Soul who did speak it forth, for the understanding and level of achievement is implicit in the words from the consciousness that they are uttered. And so, in this way, any assertions made about the Word may be viewed and understood as assertions and a reflection of the one who speaks it forth. And as well, assertions made about the Word do reflect back to the one who speaks them with a doubling of strength and effect that serves to reinforce and expand the true nature of the one who sent them forth. So, great care should always be taken to only speak the highest truth that is known and understood about the voice of Sugmad, for it does affect and can contribute to the success realized upon the path.

The Self-Realized seeker no longer has any need for active and synthetic thought, except as it is utilized to perform those calculations and tasks that do serve the higher self and its desires and needs. Instead, the seeker does become the active recipient of intuition, for this is the gift and the mechanism by which Soul communicates with the lower bodies below the Great Divide. And so, for the Self-Realized student, he always should beware and take care to keep the activity and assertions of the mind in their proper place and function, for they are not beneficial to selecting of what is the path and proper course to proceed along the way and in the direction of greater success.

With each spiritual success that is won by the student on the path, it is not uncommon to experience a commensurate rise in fear, for this is the natural defense mechanism and reaction of the mind, as it does perceive its increasing loss of control and dominion over the lower bodies of man, for each spiritual success does lead you closer to your goal and farther from the illusion that has kept you bound and chained. And fear is one of the key elements by which the heart is kept closed and the intuition and love and power from above from being heard. So, for the student with the goal of Self-Realization, this fear can be an escalating thing as the mind loses more and more control over the familiar ways and patterns that so long have been its realm and authority to command. But surrender truly is the key to surpassing the fear that grips the heart and is generated by the mind, and through surrender and vigilance and discipline and trust will the heart be truly opened and the goal be attained and realized.

The ego is the greatest obstacle to be overcome before the student may attain Self-Realization, for the ego does control the lower bodies, and it is its last gasp and fight for autonomy that does well precede Self-Realization, and the toil of this process is often called and referred to as the dark night of Soul, for in the months and possible years preceding the attainment of this great enlightened state a battle is waged within the inner bodies for control of the heart of man. And Soul and its awareness as given through the heart does battle with the ego as to whose directions and commands shall be followed as the seeker goes through life. And the ferocity of this battle often may be seen as evidenced by the turmoil and inner conflict that is felt within the heart of the student when the time does come quite near. However, the solution to the problem, as has been said before, is in trust and surrender and discipline and vigilance, for truly are these the keys that shall safely guide the seeker home and to the attainment of his goal.

The road to Self-Realization is possible alone but is more difficult and perilous without the guidance and protection of a Master who does lead from without and within the inner realms, for there are shortcuts and techniques and skills that are given by the Living Sehaji Master to those who follow him. And, as well, under the Master's protection, the karma is received and experienced at a rate that is manageable and can be successfully overcome. And finally, it is important to know and understand that many entities and dark angels do lurk in parts unseen, and it is their duty and purpose to delay all seekers on the path and aid the work of illusion and fear. And an Inner and Outer Master does give to you his protection to keep these things at bay and all delays and obstacles to a minimum.

And, as well, it is an important function of the Living Sehaji Master that he connects the energy of God and of his students between the inner and outer realms, and this does give the participants in The Way of Truth a great advantage when they do seek to follow the lines of energy and pathways to explore and learn and travel within the inner planes to visit Masters and temples where they do seek to go. So, this is all to say that there are many different reasons why it is truly a good thing to seek the Self-Realized state within the cloak of protection and understanding of one such as the Living Sehaji Master. However, it can be done alone, though this is not a method or journey I would ever recommend.

Some may think and say that Self-Realization is a sufficient level and state that is required to do what must be done and escape the Wheel of 84. Now this is not the case and should not be believed as something to be followed, for God-Realization should be the goal of every participant in The Way of Truth in this lifetime. Self-Realization is a great accomplishment and a nice thing to attain, but God-Realization is the state where the true and full powers and abilities and wisdom of the higher self begin to be understood and developed and realized. It is true that Self-Realization frees you from the lower bodies and illusions of the dual worlds. However, God-Realization connects you with the Ocean of Love and Mercy and opens your heart to wonders and wisdom and power that barely can be imagined from within the Self-Realized state. And so, for the seeker to find and experience the fullest expression and experience of what and who he truly is, he should not be satisfied with merely attaining the state of the sixth plane of the Sugmad, for God-Realization is a worthy and attainable goal and should be strived for and held as the destination for every seeker on the path, for in this way shall your ultimate truth and power be realized and experienced in this lifetime here on Earth.

(End of Paulji's discourse.)

Leytor (spoken directly and verbatim)

The purpose of this chapter is to give the student greater skills and understanding of the finer points of wisdom and truth that may be had to aid him on his way unto his destination. The heart and power of God is an attainable and true thing that may be experienced in this lifetime, if the student has the courage and discipline and vigilance to face his many fears head on and confront and overcome all challenges that are sent to him upon the path. Do not become discouraged or fear you cannot succeed, for this is not the case. Each Master who has come before you once thought as you do now, and it was his own perseverance and courage that brought him to the place in higher realms that now he does return to give what he does know and have learned to aid others on the path. So when you get discouraged and feel like giving up, do not despair, for you are loved and protected by many up above who seek only to aid in your success and endeavors.

Chapter Twelve

The Wisdom of God

The Nameless One (spoken directly and verbatim)

I am the Great God above Sugmad and above all Its brothers that run the many universes of my realms, for there is none higher than I within the conception and understanding of man. I did create, originally, the Grey and White and Beige lines to be the forces of energy within all my universes and realms and to keep the balance that is required to continue all things in their stead. From my three Sons who are the heads of these three lines were all other Souls and things created, including all Souls who do comprise the Brotherhood of the Sugmad and carry out those duties and responsibilities that do include the maintenance and function of all the universe over which It does have dominion and control. I may be called Great Father or the Nameless One, for there is not a specific name that can be held and spoken for what I am that will not contain too much power and throw the one who utters it into imbalance and certain harm.

I may be called God, though all who bear this title are somewhat identified by a misunderstood term, for God is merely the description that is given by a less developed Soul for something that it cannot fathom or understand from the point of awareness and unfoldment that it truly does possess. However, more will be said of this later, for now is not yet the time. For our purposes, and for the convenience of semantics, it can be said that I am the Nameless One, the Greatest God of all, above all others and all Souls and universes and planes of existence to include the Sugmad and all Its brothers and sisters and all who do exist above and below their realms. I am the center and primary cause and first movement of all existence and creation as it is known and understood within all my realms and universes. I AM the One, the Unity, Pure Manifestation, the Purpose and Architect of Divine Law, and embodiment of the purpose, function, and nature of existence itself. It is by my hand and intention that all exists and functions as it does within any realm where Soul may travel or exist. I love all, and my love gives the power and sustenance of life to any who experience awareness and the reality in which they are born and do create. This is I, as can be here described within the limitations of language and understanding of the human mind within the Physical Plane.

My self-reflective consciousness of the state I am is a unique perspective and understanding. I am all. I exist within all, yet I need all Souls and their individual purpose and creativity to reflect the heart and nature and essence of who and what I am. I am conscious of the state and breadth and depth of my own existence, but only in relation to what is conceived and done and enacted by those who are me and are of my body and the children of my Sons. I can know anything or nothing or everything, for I am a sea of consciousness, whereas you are Soul, a tiny speck of my cosmic universal self. I exist as a magnitude of order expanded beyond the single point, but without mass or depth or breadth, but with greater scope and power and energy. And I do draw my breath and power from realms unseen and unknowable to constantly replenish of myself and send my love and power to all great Souls below to keep the universes of existence sustained and all forever moving forward. I am the source of Soul. I am God. I am all, yet I am none. For this is the paradox of my own existence and continual journey, for without the children of my own essence to be my reflection and foil, I cannot know or see what and who I am.

The relationship of God to man is a greatly misunderstood and improperly functioning thing within the teachings of so many self-proclaimed paths to freedom. Sugmad is a Soul, like any other, like the Kal or the Nine or the Lords of Karma or Milarepa. However, Sugmad has developed and unfolded and matured and grown to a level of understanding and point of responsibility so as to have the position and mission of managing this universe of my domain below the Ocean of Love and Mercy that is Its home and dwelling.

And so, the perfect structure and relationship between God and man is one of love and learning. Soul exists because I love it, and Sugmad as well, for our love together provides the power and sustenance that keeps this and all planes within Its universe functioning. Yet Sugmad is benevolent and full of love and caring, and all that It does is done to teach the student lessons to awaken within its heart the understanding and embrace of its own true nature and capabilities. And so, the proper nature of the relationship between man and God is as that between old friends, where the one of greater knowledge and understanding does patiently guide and teach the one with less, and in this manner is love and wisdom and power shown to the younger one to aid him in his pathways and his struggles.

The attainment of God-Realization is that state where Soul has realized the level of understanding and merit that it can consciously touch and wield the pure power of the Ocean of Love and Mercy. This is a different thing in scope and magnitude and grandeur than that of the Self-Realized state, which does relate to the mastery of the lower bodies within the dual worlds below. To attain God-Realization requires a level of commitment, study and understanding that does well exceed that required to attain the Self-Realized state, yet this is a perfectly possible thing within this lifetime of the seeker, for the teachings now being brought to light do contain of perfect wisdom and truth in a degree never before available to man within the Physical Plane. And so, what once was only a dream of mystics and sages of the caves now is a possible reality for all who walk the path and are committed to its ways and the instruction and truth within this book and the many others of Dan Rin shall clearly point the way and how the trials may be overcome and the God-Realized state attained.

To carry the mantle of God-Realization in this life is a very different reality compared to the normal consciousness of man. It may be likened to peering at the heavens with the naked eye on a cloudy night versus being on the highest peak with the most powerful telescope in existence, and even then the contrast is not sufficient to adequately describe and justify this state. God-Realization is a state of such perfect clarity and understanding that all may be seen and understood, and the power of the love that

201

flows through you, you cannot help but smile and always seek to share what you do know and give to all around you to help them to the state that you do now enjoy, for it is a reality so much more interesting and stimulating and provocative than any that may be imagined from within the human consciousness of man that it is difficult to well describe the illumination and power that does embody and pertain to this mighty and high state.

The mantle of Living Sehaji Mastership was established within this universe of the Sugmad because there must be one beneath Its heart who can take a physical body and walk upon the Earth and other planets and teach all young Souls what must be known to guide them on the path and in their return home, for one of the restrictions of Sugmad's role and nature is that It may not descend within a physical shell to aid the toils and struggles of man. And so, there must be one who is nearly of Its equal to enact Its will and ways and guide Its universe in the unfoldment and cycles of Its many needs and functions. And so, the mantle of Living Sehaji Mastership was conceived and given, that a Soul of mighty merit would always exist within this universe to bridge the intention and efforts and desires between the Sugmad and all Its sons and daughters.

Wisdom is the understanding of the laws and secrets that do pertain to and unlock the secrets of Soul and of the universe. The God-Realized seeker exercises this faculty in daily life and living to do the work of Sugmad and aid others on the path and create the life that does fulfill its own desires and wishes, for wisdom is not to be kept locked away or hidden but freely shared and given to any who are ready and seek to know Its heart to aid them on their journey home. And so, the God-Realized seeker does move within his life and watch for the signs and opportunities that this is the time and place to exercise the truth that he has garnered to aid of his own cause, or Sugmad's, or any others who do need what he does know.

The God-power is the flow of energy, wisdom, love and truth from the Ocean of Love and Mercy through the heart and lower bodies of the student. It is a polarizing force that creates in the dual worlds a similarity of perfection and existence to what does lie above, yet it differs greatly in consistency, fineness, magnitude, potency and refinement from that power realized by the Soul in the Self-Realized state upon the sixth Plane of God. The analogy that can be made is that when man walks in his human consciousness, it is as if he walks upon the path of his own reality, powered only by his own two feet and personal strength and endurance. When he does reach Self-Realization, it is as if he has learned to drive a car, and when he does reach the God-Realized state, it is as if he does have and drive his own personal spaceship that can take him in an instant to any place he could think of or ever desire to be. Such is the difference in nature and power of the various realized states.

And so, one could ask, "What do I need a spaceship for, if I am content to walk on Earth or perhaps travel a bit more quickly if I can have a car?" And this is a perfectly valid and justifiable question and one that should be honored and respected. However, the worthy Soul should also consider this: Existence is an adventure. This is its purpose and function, to learn and grow and explore and have new and enjoyable experiences and to help others to do the same. So, as the Soul does mature and begin to understand and master its powers and the abilities that do accompany its own true state and nature, the spaceship does soon become the desired means of travel. And so, for the God-Realized, the exercise of his power does fall within the activities of everyday life and living, yet now he has the understanding and ability to proactively shape and create the entire reality that is his own, and this is a powerful and enjoyable and desirable position to always find oneself in.

The power of man and of his organizations cannot compare in scope or strength to the God-power wielded by the seeker. Man-power is structured and operates on the premise of physical cause and effect. That is to say, looking for and creating action in the physical realm to enact the physical effect that is desired. And so, any manifestation that does occur is merely a side effect and haphazard by-product of other forces unseen and misunderstood. God-power, by contrast, is the utilization of the stuff and raw material of existence to, with the imagination and spiritual skills and techniques, manifest the reality of your choosing with far less physical exertion and wasted energy than that of man's limited view from within the human consciousness and organization, for one does use the low vibration power of the pinda realm and the other does use the high, pure source that creates of all below, and this is the difference between the two and their nature and true function.

Love is an oft-maligned and misunderstood word and concept within the lower realms and much has been already said on the topic in this and other places. However, the purpose of this teaching is of how to love man as God. Each man you do encounter is to be looked to and regarded as a close and beloved friend of old, for each you do encounter is only a vehicle to bring you the love and wisdom of Sugmad's heart and teaching, either to teach you a lesson that you do need to know to progress farther on the path, to receive from you a teaching, which is your honor and gift to have that sacred opportunity to earn more merit and the trust of the Sugmad, or to bring into your life greater love and support and understanding for the many trials you face and to aid you on the path and the way of your own journeys. So, any way that you can evaluate the situation and look at its own heart does require a position of love and appreciation and compassion for all who cross your path, for each is an instrument and vessel for God and should always be treated as such.

Mankind should always strive for a love for all others that can be described as detached goodwill and grace. Certainly there are those within your life to whom you will have greater bonds of affection and affinity than to those whom you have never met, and this is true wherever you go within any of the universes of my realms, for Souls do, over time, develop stronger connections with those with whom they often do come in contact and proceed along the path. And so, the intensity and closeness and nature of the love and affection that is born between two Souls, such as these, may differ in character and essence than between two who have never met, yet to each, even unto the strangers, a love of detached goodwill and compassion should be given to aid them on the path and grant them the grace and freedom to proceed unimpeded along the way that they have chosen for their own journey on the road. And this is the type of love mankind should strive for in his daily toils and travels.

Of love, wisdom, and power, the three aspects and characteristics of God-Realization, love is the most important because without love neither of the latter may be achieved or understood. Love is the key to opening of the heart and intuition and to the doors to higher realms where wisdom and power may be acquired and obtained. And so, though these are important things to the balanced development and progression of the Soul for the early seeker on the path, or one not well versed and educated in esoteric lore or understanding, love is the simple thing to be remembered, for it is truly the key and base foundation upon which all other achievement is built in the cathedral of God-power that is constructed by each Soul as its own reality and works.

I created Soul for the very simple reason that often has been told: to know myself. I am a Spirit of Consciousness and Power and Wisdom, but without anything to peer at and gaze I was an undifferentiated pool of Is-ness and needed some external thing to be my mirror and reflection, for perspective is truly relative to the thing that is being perceived. And so, without Soul, I was unable to see or know myself or experience the nature of my own being and essence. And so, originally, I did create Soul and gave it a perfect garden paradise in a universe from my dreaming and all did enjoy the endless bounty of my heart, yet within me something stirred that was of a different nature, and I did realize that there was an element of struggle that was necessary to temper and refine myself as Soul to a greater level of refinement and responsibility. And so, though it was no fault of those who lived below in the paradise I had created, I did create the dual worlds through my three sons of old, and into these new worlds were all Souls sent to go and learn and mature and remember their own nature. And thus were the cycles initiated, and the great game was begun that was creation, sustenance, and destruction, as is the way and truth that creates the many circumstances of constantly changing nature that does propel all Souls upon the path. And I am most satisfied and happy with my creations, for I now do see and know the wide breadth and scope of actions that I am capable of, and this has and does give me the truth and understanding I had sought to know of my own Self.

The physical universe was the last step in the creation of the lower dual worlds, as a place for Souls to go and learn of their own eternal nature, for it is the lowest in vibration that the positive and negative energies can sink to and still exist. And so, this coarse and cold and dense barren plane of reality was constructed to provide to man the harshest of all conditions in which to make his home and learn the lessons of his true eternal self and nature, for I did perceive within myself that it was a necessary and good thing for Soul to be able to survive and flourish under even the most difficult of conditions, for life within the inner planes above the physical world is of ease and comfort by comparison. And like the soldier does go through the trials and rigors of boot camp and great training and conditioning to become prepared for the moment of truth and the test of true discipline and ability, so too does Soul endure the rigors of the Physical Plane and successfully pass all challenges and master its own self and abilities before it is prepared to go and face the greater challenges above. For the discipline and wisdom and love required to be Sugmad and manage an entire universe is a somewhat greater thing than the attainment of Self-Realization below. And so, the physical world was constructed and does function to prepare all Souls and train them for the challenges and toils that do await it above.

Soul is not so very different from God, as might be thought and understood. Certainly there are differences in scope and ability and breadth of understanding and strength of power, but in its essential characteristics and qualities and tendencies, Soul and God do share much in common, for when man does act and walk and perceive from his higher nature and aspect, then he is indeed very close and similar to God.

The final steps between the upper rungs on the ladder of God-Realization are not so far apart as one would suppose. This is why when one does look upon or become close to any who are considered saints or saviors or illumined Masters of the way, they are often not so different seeming in character and habit as you or any other, for God is the Father of Soul, and Soul is created in Its likeness, and this is a literal statement from the point of view of the consciousness. Certainly, the physical form and characteristics do vary among the many Souls of many places, but the characteristics

206

of awareness, perception, is-ness, beingness and wisdom are quite closely similar to God. So, when you do feel disheartened or frustrated with your progress, do remember that you are already made in the likeness and image of God, for your creator and your Father is closer to you than you do know, and the love It bears you truly is a reflection of the esteem with which It does hold Its own self.

God is law unto Itself. This is both Its perception and the fact of existence, although there is one limitation. God may not violate the free will of Soul. In every other respect Its power and word is law, but not in this consideration, for otherwise it would be too great a temptation to merely alter the free will of Soul, whenever the situation did arise that suited necessary conditions. Because love is the law of existence, this is why this limitation is imposed, for it does force all within the heavens to seek another way and solution for any problem that does arise, for if the violation of free will and use of force is forbidden to resolve of different situations, then love and compassion and creativity are the ways that remain to do what must be done. And so, in every other aspect, God is a law unto Itself in all the realms and planes below the level of Its initiation and mantle, for there always does exist within all my universes and planes one who is higher in merit and power and whose own word does exceed your own. However, within the domains of Sugmad's realms and all planets, places, heavens and hells, within Its borders and planes, the Word of Sugmad is law unto Itself for whatever It does say and wish to do.

All Souls were given inviolable free will while within the physical realm. This may not be the case, however, within the higher realms, for as Soul does finally find itself freed of the lower planes and does ascend to realms above to begin its duties there, it must agree to abide the law and word of those above its rank in merit and achievement, for in this way is all order and functioning achieved within the pure worlds above. However, the Soul does have a choice, and if it does desire to live a life of exercising its own free will, regardless of the desires or plans of Sugmad or other Masters, then it is free to descend again and continue its lives on Earth, for in the inner worlds, each and every Soul does serve within one Hierarchy or Order or another and as part of that line or organization is bound to obey the word and commands of those above it in merit and initiation. That is not to say that the commands and wishes of higher Souls are not sometimes disobeyed, for this is truly the case, and in these instances, Soul is sent below again to learn once more the lessons that it might act in proper ways and with proper respect and action. Do not think, however, that this means all within the inner realms are bound and slaves to those above them, for this is not the case. Each Soul is given great latitude and freedom to do as it does please in fulfilling its mission and purpose. But in the rare instances, when one of greater merit does appear and requests of certain actions or behaviors, this is a request to be obeyed, lest it does become a command. Rarely, however, is this a necessary step to take, for Soul within the higher realms does have a much greater perspective and understanding of the interrelationships and forces that do make all actions necessary. And so, in most if not all the cases, a simple request does suffice to accomplish the desired goal. However, in the rare instance that the request is not heeded, the Soul of lesser accomplishment and merit is truly bound to obey, unless it does desire to return to realms below and continue in its hardships and training.

So upon the Physical Plane, all mankind does possess inviolable free will, and this does include how man does treat and react to those sent to do Its will and ways, for those who represent my will on Earth, or the will of the Sugmad, which is for all intents and purposes the same in most matters, do come to bring the truth of liberation to man. Yet often he does react negatively to the presence of the one who comes to set him free, for the mind does fear the liberation of the lower self by Soul and the eradication of its position of importance.

And so, for Soul to learn the difficult lessons it must master, it is given free will to act as it desires within the Physical Plane, although it does suffer the karmic consequences of the errors of its way. And so, too, do all the Masters who come and serve below do so out of a great love for man and all Souls who struggle on the path, for compared to their existence and pleasurable home in realms above, the hardships and dangers and difficulties of an incarnation here on Earth are only born out of a great love and compassion for all who live and breathe and struggle on the path.

The test and journey of Soul is to learn to live this life and fully trust in my unfailing love for you, as given through the heart of the Sugmad. And this can be a difficult thing to do, for ignorance and fear created by misunderstanding and the mind do surely cloud the vision and wisdom of the heart. And many forces do conspire to keep you from my love and the freedom that is won when realms above are attained and the real journey and adventure begun. So, to the seeker on the path and bound by the physical shell and world of illusions, I do say this: Trust in love and the wisdom and teachings that are given by the Living Sehaji Master, and do the exercises and techniques as they are sent to you, and in this way shall your heart gradually grow and open to the unfailing love and guidance that I do offer you to aid you in your journeys to successfully return back home to my heart.

Complete surrender is the key to God-Realization and the access to the God worlds. The Soul must learn to trust and abide the ways and laws of my heart as they are taught and given to him, for only through the understanding and demonstration and embodiment of my own nature and truth shall you achieve the goal you seek. Human will and decisions cannot ever lead the seeker home to God, for the mind is not capable to know and guide you to the thing that so exceeds it. And so, it is only by trust and surrender and abidance of my way and laws, as understood and given through the heart, that God-Realization may be attained in the fullness and grandeur and power of its realm.

The Light and Sound of God is woven as threads of gold in every theology and path that has ever been taught on Earth, for the teachings that have been given and received and shared by prophets and saviors throughout the ages of man have each contained that segment of truth that was appropriate to the next level and stage of development that was needed to take that group or culture to the next step and stage along the path. And so, the Light and Sound has been given in discrete units that could be understood and were appropriate to the time and place and culture in which they were received.

The culmination of all paths and the gateway to the Ocean of Love and Mercy is through the teachings of The Way of Truth, for in this final age of man the highest truth is finally given and shared in a comprehensive and complete way that does contain the golden thread and bridge from all other paths and ways to finally return the Soul to the heart of the Sugmad.

Each way of life and path that is productive and based on teachings of love does stand on its own merit and deserves respect and the freedom of judgment by others, for each way and path contains the Light and Sound in the measure and degree that is appropriate for the stage and level of development and unfoldment of the one who follows its ways. It is to the free will and discretion of the seeker on the path to select the teachings that do ring true within his heart to guide him on the next stage of his journey, and each of you in The Way of Truth has, at some time in the past, walked that path and way, or one that was very similar, to finally arrive at the place where you now are. So, the test of detachment and compassion is to give each Soul the grace and each way and path the respect and freedom from judgment that each does truly deserve, as a worthy and necessary component of the complete journey and quest for God.

To say that without the Godman nothing could exist is a truth that must be pondered and understood, for the Godman can mean different things to those at different places on the path, and the determination of its meaning is the key to understanding this truth. In this case, the Godman does mean the Living Sehaji Master, and without him nothing could exist within this universe of the Sugmad. The Godman, the Living Sehaji Master, is the conduit and path for truth and the creative inspiration and urgings of all who walk and live and contribute to the construction of all realms and planes below. Through the mantle of the Godman, through the seventeenth plane, does pass all God-power on its way from the Ocean of Love and Mercy to the lower planes below, and it is received by the Living Sehaji Master as it does come from the Sugmad, and then through the love of the Living Sehaji Master, it is passed to realms below to power all existence within the universe of Its heart.

And so, it is a true thing to say that without the Godman or the Soul that bears that mantle of the seventeenth plane of God, there could not exist any universe of the Sugmad or any of Its brothers, by the one who plays a similar role in their universes of their own. And so, the Godman is the gift from my heart to all my children in all my universes, to enable the creation of all the worlds below and to guide all seekers to the truth and return them to their home in the heavens above.

The ignorance and fear and misunderstanding of my children in realms below does cause great and unnecessary suffering and pain to many who do bring upon others the result of their own hurt and improper actions; and so, I give to you this poem to aid all to carry on and find strength and love and compassion to truly overcome the difficulties and trials each does face.

"When each does walk upon the path,
And encounters painful struggles.
A heart of love and compassion too,
May be a rare thing to find.
But grace and warmth and truth of life,
Never can be defeated.
If you do carry your head high,
And not allow its weakness.
For love and strength and compassion all,
Are characteristics of the Father.
And I do smile when my children below,
Do remember of my teachings.
So do not fear or strike to harm,
When you are hurt and reeling.
From the ignorance that is sown,
To keep you from your healing.
I have sent my words below,
To aid the heart and seeing.
Read these my truths and you shall know,
The only way to achieving,
The goal of your true heart."

This shall be the poem to inspire strength and love and compassion to all upon the path.

When the seeker does finally arrive at the heaven of heavens within the worlds beyond the Sugmad, the bliss and joy of the experience of sitting at the knee of the Masters and others who do teach there is indescribable and beyond the capability of comprehension to any who walk the Earth. And for those few Souls who toil on and cease not in their strivings and finally succeed in entering through the door to my heart to sit at my knee and hear my words and truth of understanding is the goal and highest honor that ever can be achieved within any universe in all my realms and existence, for the love that is felt and poured from my heart and into that of the seeker is of such fineness and purity and intensity that it would, in an instant, burn the Sugmad to a cinder were the full power of its torrent unleashed into the Ocean of Love and Mercy. But this is to be the goal and final destination of all Souls within the universes, for my heart and home is the final place where all great Souls do come and finally rest and learn and teach until their next assignment to show others who do follow them the way to return back home.

As participants in The Way of Truth and travelers on the path to the bosom of Sugmad above, it is the task and true challenge to maintain the divine consciousness moment-by-moment each day, for this does go beyond mere neutrality and detachment, but to being a conscious conduit and servant of Sugmad to manifest Its love and power in every act that is done and every facet of one's life. And so, to maintain the divine connection, eternal vigilance must be had to every moment see the truth and opportunity to serve and see of Sugmad's ways and wishes in any you do meet and do encounter, for each thing, person and circumstance that is met on the path is an opportunity to see and learn and express the divine consciousness that is the sight behind the veil in the dual planes below. So my final advice in this matter is to always hold within your heart and awareness the presence of divine love and power in all you see and do, and this shall speed you on your way and your return to the Holy Spirit above.

My words have here been given for the first time on the Earth to tell all seekers the truth and give to them the understanding to aid them on their journey home in this final age of man. The way has been long and painful for many who do come, and it is to your

213

everlasting merit that you do continue to forge on and not fall or be slowed or stopped by fear and the illusions that you do encounter on the path. These words have opened the doorway to other truths that shall follow on and still be given by the writings of the Living Sehaji Master. The everlasting truth of my heart, which never is to be forgotten, is of the infinite power of love, for if there is but one thing that always is remembered it is this: Love is the only way and the true path to my heart, and this is the most important thing that could be said to any who aspires and seeks his true home in the heavens above. This is all of the true teachings to be given at this time. I await you up above with hope and anticipation.

May peace and love be with you.

INDEX

A

Abbott, 27
Agam Des, 96
Age of man, 83
Age of Mind, 54, 83, 111
Age of Soul (Heart), 83, 112
Astral,
  Cities:
  Anda Pad or Turiya Pad, 12
    Ruler, Kal Niranjan
  Narat, 12
  Net Le Por, 13=]
  Pel To Let, 14
    Master, Bran Lanat, 14
  Teret Ya, 13
  Plane, 11-14, 29, 83, 181
  Temples:
  Narlat Tre, 12
  Neranjala, 12
  Peren Te Let, 13
  Trenet, 14
  Unitem Brevi, 14
  Vortex:
  Astral, 12-14
Attitude, 135, 137
Awareness, 57-59, 61, 63, 80,
  105, 125, 128-129, 146,
  163, 165, 170-171, 179-
  184, 195-196, 199-200,
  207, 213

B

Balance, 3, 5-6, 8-10, 15, 19-20,
  24-30, 32, 36-37, 49-51, 53-
  55, 60, 63, 65-66, 71, 73-
  74, 77-78, 82, 85, 101-103,
  105-106, 110, 112, 119-
  123, 127-130, 134-137,
  141, 146, 150, 153-154,
  158-159, 167, 170-174, 76,
  183-185, 190-194, 199, 205

Balance continued:
  Imbalance, 6, 50, 53, 60,
    66, 73, 101-102, 103,
    105, 122, 173, 199
  Of universe, 13, 24, 35-36,
    39, 46, 49
  Rebalance, 190
Best-laid plans, 9, 22, 24, 26-27,
  49, 51, 53-54, 65, 100, 115,
  127, 131-132, 135, 140-
  141, 146, 151, 161, 163
Brahm, 5-6, 8, 10, 28
Brakosani Order, 27

C

Causal
  Cities:
  Brahma Lok, 10
    Ruler: Brahm
  Bret Lor, 10
  Kep Na Tor, 11
  Trek Nor, 11
  Plane, 10, 29, 83, 181
  Temples:
  Mek Le Tor, 10
  Tret Fer, 11
  Vortex:
  Causal, 11
  Brahm (guardian), 10
Celestial Seas, 27
Compassion, 10, 59, 72-73, 75,
  112, 122, 129, 147, 149,
  152-153, 162, 165, 174,
  204, 207-208, 210-212
Consciousness, 7, 14, 18, 27, 35,
  44-45, 47, 50, 53, 57-59,
  61, 63, 80, 83, 85-86, 89,
  97, 99-100, 106, 112, 115,
  125, 128,   132-136, 141,
  145, 162-163, 165, 169,
  171, 180, 191-192, 195,
  200-201,203-206, 213

215

H
Heart, 1, 7, 10, 15, 17,-18, 28-29,
41, 44, 48-50, 54, 58-59,
66, 69-73, 76-83, 88-89, 91,
93-97, 99, 105-109, 117,
119, 122-124, 126-130,
135-142, 145-160, 162-166,
168-169, 172, 174-180,
188, 190-191, 194, 196-
198, 200-202, 204-205,
207, 209-214
Heaven(s), 3, 6, 7, 11-12, 16, 19-
20, 27, 30, 40, 42-43, 46,
54-55, 59-60, 88, 92, 95,
98, 101, 106, 109-111, 113,
117, 149, 151, 155, 161,
167, 172, 178-179, 201,
207, 211, 213-214
Holy Spirit, 32, 40-41, 43-45, 55,
66, 81-82, 88, 94, 97, 99-
100, 103-105, 107, 124-
125, 127-129, 132-134,
138-139, 142, 147, 150-
151, 159, 164, 167, 172-
173,175, 185, 187, 189,
195, 213
HU *See* Mantra,
Humility, 46, 112, 147, 152

I
Illumination, 90, 101, 202
Illusion, 19, 59-61, 63-66, 69-74,
80, 90-91, 94, 102-105,
107, 109-111, 115, 124,
136-138, 142, 146, 148,
150, 157, 162-164, 166,
176, 182-183, 191, 194,
196-198, 209, 214. *See
also* Maya
Imagination, 6, 67, 69, 80-82, 85-
86, 110, 159, 166, 169, 186,
203

Initiation, 22, 24-25, 29, 32, 37,
39, 44, 50-53, 70, 86, 90,
94-95, 103, 110, 148, 162,
173, 179-180, 184, 186,
188, 190,192, 207-208
2nd, 38, 40, 104
5th, 86, 89
6th, 86
8th, 51, 90
9th, 51
10th, 42, 52
11th, 52
12th, 52
13th, 52
14th, 52-53
15th, 53
16th, 53
Intuition, 48, 165, 191, 196, 205

K
Kal-power, 124, 136
Kali Yuga, 14-15, 111
Karma and karmic, 14, 30-33,
42-43, 48, 63-64, 70, 75,
77-78, 80, 86, 103, 107,
119-121, 126-127, 129,
131-132, 135, 140-141,
152-153, 169, 175, 197, 208
Debts, 30, 32, 76, 82, 106,
130, 140, 163, 190
Law of, 135-136, 150
Negative, 13
Neutral, 63, 72, 79, 82, 136
Patterns, 74, 126
Signatures, 78
Knowledge, 4, 8, 12, 14, 18, 21,
23, 25, 30, 38-39, 44, 58,
61, 63, 88-89, 91, 127, 132-
133, 142, 152, 157, 160-
161, 181, 187, 194, 201

221

223